OPRAH
WINFREY

The African-American Biographies series

MAYA ANGELOU
More Than a Poet
0-89490-684-4

LOUIS ARMSTRONG
King of Jazz
0-89490-997-5

ARTHUR ASHE
Breaking the Color Barrier
in Tennis
0-89490-689-5

BENJAMIN BANNEKER
Astronomer and Mathematician
0-7660-1208-5

RALPH BUNCHE
Winner of the Nobel Peace Prize
0-7660-1203-4

W. E. B. DU BOIS
Champion of Civil Rights
0-7660-1209-3

DUKE ELLINGTON
Giant of Jazz
0-89490-691-7

ARETHA FRANKLIN
Motown Superstar
0-89490-686-0

WHOOPI GOLDBERG
Comedian and Movie Star
0-7660-1205-0

LORRAINE HANSBERRY
Playwright and Voice of Justice
0-89490-945-2

LANGSTON HUGHES
Poet of the
Harlem Renaissance
0-89490-815-4

ZORA NEALE HURSTON
Southern Storyteller
0-89490-685-2

QUINCY JONES
Musician, Composer, Producer
0-89490-814-6

BARBARA JORDAN
Congresswoman, Lawyer,
Educator
0-89490-692-5

CORETTA SCOTT KING
Striving for
Civil Rights
0-89490-811-1

MARTIN LUTHER KING, JR.
Leader for Civil Rights
0-89490-687-9

TONI MORRISON
Nobel Prize-Winning
Author
0-89490-688-7

WALTER DEAN MYERS
Writer for Real Teens
0-7660-1206-9

JESSE OWENS
Track and Field Legend
0-89490-812-X

COLIN POWELL
Soldier and Patriot
0-89490-810-3

PAUL ROBESON
Actor, Singer,
Political Activist
0-89490-944-4

JACKIE ROBINSON
Baseball's Civil Rights
Legend
0-89490-690-9

IDA B. WELLS-BARNETT
Crusader Against Lynching
0-89490-947-9

OPRAH WINFREY
Talk Show Legend
0-7660-1207-7

CARTER G. WOODSON
Father of African-American History
0-89490-946-0

—African-American Biographies—

OPRAH WINFREY

Talk Show Legend

Series Consultant:
Dr. Russell L. Adams, Chairman
Department of Afro-American Studies, Howard University

Sara McIntosh Wooten

Enslow Publishers, Inc.

40 Industrial Road	PO Box 38
Box 398	Aldershot
Berkeley Heights, NJ 07922	Hants GU12 6BP
USA	UK

http://www.enslow.com

Library of Congress Cataloging-in-Publication Data

Wooten, Sara McIntosh.
    Oprah Winfrey : talk show legend / Sara McIntosh Wooten.
      p. cm. — (African-American biographies)
    Includes bibliographical references and index.
    Summary: A biography of the performer and talk show host, discussing her childhood of neglect and her rise to the top of the entertainment world.
    ISBN 0-7660-1207-7
    1. Winfrey, Oprah—Juvenile literature. 2. Television personalities—United States—Biography—Juvenile literature. 3. Motion picture actors and actresses—United States—Biography—Juvenile literature. 4. Afro-American women—Biography—Juvenile literature. [1. Winfrey, Oprah. 2. Television personalities. 3. Actors and actresses. 4. Afro-Americans—Biography. 5. Women—Biography.] I. Title. II. Series.
PN1992.4.W56W68   1999
791.45'028'092
[b] —DC21   98-27770
                                           CIP
                                           AC

Printed in the United States of America

10 9 8 7 6 5 4 3 2

To Our Readers: All Internet addresses in this book were active and appropriate when we went to press. Any comments or suggestions can be sent by e-mail to Comments@enslow.com or to the address on the back cover.

Illustration Credits: AP/Wide World Photos, pp. 93, 103; Courtesy of ABC7/Chicago, WLS-TV, Chicago, IL, p. 51; Courtesy of Photofest, pp. 57, 68, 73, 82, 97; Courtesy of Metropolitan Government Archives, Nashville, TN, pp. 15, 37, 40; Courtesy of the Milwaukee Public Library, Milwaukee, WI, p. 23; Everett Collection, pp. 11, 52, 61, 110; Joseph Langone, p. 104; Kosciusko, MS Chamber of Commerce, p. 20; Peter Sokop, p. 114; Sara Wooten, pp. 29, 33, 79.

Cover Illustration: AP/Wide World Photos

CONTENTS

Acknowledgments

The author wishes to thank Willa Sanders for her help and generosity with Kosciusko, Mississippi, pictures; Eddy Gonzalez for her speedy archives search; Margaret L. Jones, Katherine Sneed, and Polly Sheldon for their insights and recollections; Linda Center and Debbie Cox for their assistance at the Nashville, Tennessee, Metropolitan Government Archives; and Jim and Carrie Wooten for their willingness to endure Mom's obsession.

1

DAY OF DISASTER

t was April Fool's Day, 1977. Oprah Winfrey was just twenty-three years old. She did not know it yet, but she was about to face one of the most difficult times of her life.

For the past seven months, Winfrey had been a coanchor on the six o'clock evening news for WJZ-TV in Baltimore, Maryland. The show was seen by thousands of people in the Baltimore area and had brought Winfrey a lot of attention. Her face beamed from billboards throughout the city. But on April 1, 1977, Oprah Winfrey's boss at WJZ-TV asked to meet with her. Winfrey's career as a rising star in the world of news broadcasting was coming to a sudden, crashing end.

For Winfrey, things had not been going very well. For one thing, some people at the station thought she never should have been hired at all.[1] At that time, Baltimore's television audiences were not used to seeing an African-American woman reporting the news every night. Some people at WJZ-TV feared that viewers might decide to turn to another station instead.

There were other problems as well. The staff at WJZ-TV did not like the way Winfrey reported the news. She did not simply read the news from the TelePrompTer as other broadcasters did. Instead, she often used her own words and reported the news in her own way. That made her stories sound more informal than the station wanted.

Still another problem was that Winfrey's feelings kept getting in the way of her news reports. People at that time expected news reporters to stay detached from their stories and to report the facts without showing any emotion at all. But when Winfrey reported tragic news stories, she could not hide how they made her feel. Her audience could tell if a story made her angry or sad.[2] As she said later, "I really was not cut out for the news. I'd have to fight back the tears if a story was too sad. I just did not have the detachment."[3] Many people at WJZ-TV thought that Winfrey's behavior was unprofessional.

As if those problems were not enough, Winfrey and her coanchor, Jerry Turner, did not work well together. Instead of cooperating with each other, they had differences in style and experience that caused problems. The strain of their partnership soon became clear to television viewers as well.[4] Winfrey was the newcomer. Turner had been a popular news anchor long before Winfrey's arrival. It was an uncomfortable situation.

With all these problems, the managers of WJZ-TV had to do something. Now, on April 1, 1977, they told Winfrey that she could not continue as the six o'clock news coanchor. Starting that very evening, she would be replaced by Al Sanders, a reporter known and liked by Baltimore audiences.

Suddenly, Winfrey's world turned upside down. Just the day before, she had been a Baltimore celebrity. Her face was known to television viewers throughout the area. Now what would she do?

Although Winfrey could not see the future on that awful April Fool's Day, a new opportunity was waiting just around the corner. That day, and the bleak days that followed, would become a path leading to a success she never could have dreamed possible.

A new station manager, Bill Carter, had just taken over at WJZ-TV. He wanted to try a new kind of program at the station. As an experiment, he wanted to see whether a morning talk-interview show would be popular with Baltimore viewers.

The show Carter planned would host only people from Baltimore as its guests. He thought viewers would like the show because it would help them get to know people, events, and issues of the city. The new talk show, premiering in 1978, would be called *People Are Talking*.

Unlike today, when talk shows are common on all the major television stations, there were far fewer to choose from in the seventies. The most well-known talk show was *The Donahue Show,* hosted by Phil Donahue. It had become very popular with audiences across the nation and had the highest ratings of any daytime television talk show at that time.

Bill Carter wanted to air *People Are Talking* at the same time as *The Donahue Show*. It would be very tough competition for *People Are Talking*, but he wanted to give it a try. Carter also thought the show should have two hosts. One would be Richard Sher, a Baltimore native with experience in broadcasting. For the other cohost, Bill Carter wanted to try Oprah Winfrey. With the show's tough time slot and Winfrey's dismal beginning at the station, many people at WJZ-TV thought Winfrey might fail at that job, too. As she later reflected, "They put me on the talk show just to get rid of me."[5]

Yet with *People Are Talking*, Winfrey found the job for which she had been born. As the show gained

Being fired from her job as a television news reporter turned out to be a terrific stroke of luck for Oprah Winfrey. She was much better suited to her next job—hosting a television talk show.

momentum with its Baltimore viewers, Winfrey felt comfortable letting her personality shine through. Winfrey's personal warmth is exactly what made her so successful as an interviewer. She really listened to the people she interviewed. She did not get distracted thinking about what her next question would be. She also seemed to know what kinds of questions to ask. The questions Winfrey asked her guests were the ones her audiences wanted answered. As she said, "I ask the questions that they want to know, because I also want to know them."[6]

With *People Are Talking*, Winfrey was a hit. From her perspective, "The first day I did it, I thought, 'This is what I really should have been doing all along.'"[7] *People Are Talking* began to beat *The Donahue Show*'s ratings with the Baltimore television audience.

Losing her job on April 1 changed Winfrey's life forever. That ending led to the beginning of her new career as a talk show host. And from that came Winfrey's spectacular rise to become the most popular and loved talk show host on the air. In the coming years, Oprah Winfrey's influence through her talk show, personal example, and sense of mission in helping others would have an impact on her fans all over the world.

2

A GIFTED CHILD

n the heart of the Deep South, the tiny town of Kosciusko, Mississippi, is about seventy miles northeast of Jackson, the state capital. On January 29, 1954, most people in Kosciusko were unaware of the birth of the community's newest resident. They had no idea of the fame she would one day bring to their obscure little town just by being born there. For it was on that day that Oprah Gail Winfrey entered the world.

Oprah Winfrey was named for Orpah, a little-known character found in the Book of Ruth in the Bible. Oprah's name was misspelled by accident on her birth certificate. With that mistake it was changed forever from Orpah to "Oprah."

Oprah was born into a very poor family. Her mother, Vernita Lee, was just eighteen years old when Oprah was brought into the world with the help of a midwife. Oprah's father, Vernon Winfrey, was in the Army. He was stationed at Fort Rucker, an Army base about 250 miles from Kosciusko. He and Vernita knew each other just a short time, and they never married.

Oprah lived with her mother and grandmother, Hattie Mae Lee. Together they made their home on what Winfrey remembers as Hattie Mae's "little bitty" farm in the countryside on the outskirts of Kosciusko.[1] On the farm they raised pigs, chickens, and cows, and they grew just enough crops for the little family to use.

When Oprah was four, Vernita Lee decided to go north to find a better job. Times were hard just then in Kosciusko. The cotton mill that provided work for many of the townspeople had closed, and jobs were scarce. Vernita Lee thought she should move to a large northern city where unskilled African-American women could find work as maids. She made up her mind to go to Milwaukee, Wisconsin, more than one thousand miles away. When her mother left Kosciusko, Oprah stayed behind on the farm with Hattie Mae Lee.

Money was always scarce in the Lee household. They could not afford to have running water in their

Vernon Winfrey, Oprah's father.

little house, and Oprah remembers watching her grandmother wash clothes by boiling them in a huge iron pot in the yard.² With no running water, the Lees used an outhouse for their bathroom.

Not even having a bed of her own, Oprah slept in a feather bed with her grandmother every night. To save money, Hattie Mae sewed all of Oprah's clothes by hand. Oprah went barefoot in the hot Mississippi weather because she had no "everyday" shoes to wear. Her only shoes during the first years of her life were a pair of shiny black patent leathers, which were saved for Sundays.

The Lees had no television, either. Instead, Oprah had the farm animals to entertain her. Sometimes she rode on the back of one of the pigs. She also talked to the animals and gave them all names. As she grew older, she read to them and told them the Bible stories that she learned in Sunday school.

Even with the farm animals to keep her company, Oprah was often lonely for other children to play with. Still, she found ways to make her own fun, and she developed her imagination at the same time. Because there was no extra money to buy toys, Oprah created toys from things she found around the house. For example, her doll was made from a corncob.

Little Oprah grew up in a culture in which children were "seen but not heard." Hattie Mae saw it as her duty to teach Oprah to behave and mind her elders.

Hattie Mae knew that life for an African-American girl in the Deep South could be dangerous, so she taught Oprah to be careful about her behavior and to show courtesy and respect to adults.

Hattie Mae's discipline included switchings. In fact, Oprah remembers being hit practically every day. Oprah knew she was in trouble when she heard Hattie Mae's order to go find a switch. That meant she had to go outside, pull a small branch off a tree, and bring it to her grandmother to whip her with. As Oprah tells it, "She could whip me for days and never get tired."[3]

Oprah also remembers sometimes wishing she had been born white instead of black. From what she saw, white children lived in better homes and had more toys than black children. They even had television sets. She also thought white children did not get switchings.[4]

Still, despite her strict discipline, Hattie Mae loved Oprah, and Oprah felt that love. She fondly remembers one time, during a frightening thunderstorm, her grandmother holding her as they stood together on the front porch. As they listened to the sound of heavy raindrops on the porch's tin roof, Oprah remembers Hattie Mae soothing her fears and assuring her that "God don't mess with his children."[5]

As Oprah grew older, Hattie Mae gave her chores to help out around the farm. Her main jobs were to feed the chickens and pigs every day and to lead the cows out to the pasture. She also carried heavy buckets of water about one hundred yards from the well to the house each day for the family to use.

Hattie Mae was convinced that in addition to discipline, Oprah needed to get an education. Although she never went to school herself, Hattie Mae had learned to read and do simple arithmetic through the years. As Oprah later explained, "She certainly was not an educated woman, but she taught me the shape of letters and she taught me my Bible stories."[6] She also read to her granddaughter and taught her the basics of reading. Soon Oprah was starting to read and write.

When she was five years old, Oprah started kindergarten in nearby Buffalo, Mississippi. But because of all she had learned from Hattie Mae, she soon found kindergarten boring. One day, she wrote a note to her teacher, saying: "Dear Miss New. I do not think I belong here."[7] Miss New agreed and soon moved Oprah into the first grade.

Despite Oprah's simple daily routine, it was a hard life for most African Americans growing up in the Deep South in the 1950s. Racist groups such as the Ku Klux Klan were active. They terrorized African Americans with threats, beatings, and even lynchings—murder by a mob.

The Lees, like many others, developed a strong religious faith to help them cope with such difficult and uncertain times. Hattie Mae had a deep reverence for God and firmly instilled her faith in Oprah. Under Hattie Mae's direction, Sundays were especially important in the rhythm of Oprah's early childhood. Every Sunday the Lees attended Buffalo United Methodist Church. It was an all-day affair, beginning with Sunday school that lasted for two hours. After that came the main church service, which continued for three more hours. At four o'clock the congregation gathered for a picnic, then returned to the church for another service in the evening.

It was a long day for an active little girl to be quiet and sit still. Oprah remembers the soft swishing of handheld paper fans, and the threatening wasps that circled overhead as she sat through services in the sticky heat of the Mississippi summers. Hattie Mae also taught Oprah to pray. Oprah remembers her grandmother's words as they knelt together: "As long as God allows you to bend, you bend."[8] Oprah would continue the practice throughout her life.

Oprah also began to memorize poems and Bible stories. She later credited Hattie Mae with "developing my natural talents early."[9] Little Oprah had gotten her first chance to entertain others at church on Easter Sunday, just a few months after her third birthday. That was when Oprah took to the stage for the first time, reciting her memorized version of the Easter story, titled "Jesus Rose on Easter Day." The adults in the congregation were amazed and delighted with the toddler's performance. Her success that day quickly led to other performances. Over time Oprah was in great demand, providing the entertainment for ladies' teas and church programs. As she later described herself, "I was always a very articulate child."[10]

While her audiences became aware of her talent and speaking presence, Oprah began to learn about herself. She loved being onstage, where her intelligence and personality could shine and develop.

Three-year-old Oprah Winfrey gave her first stage performance here at the Buffalo United Methodist Church in Kosciusko, Mississippi. Little Oprah had memorized the Easter story, much to the delight of everyone in church that day.

Others might be terrified at the thought of speaking before a crowd of people, but Oprah thrived on the attention. "Everywhere I went, I'd say, 'Do you want to hear me do something?'"[11] At the conclusion of her presentations, she would curtsy or bow, delighting the audience with her confidence and flair. Before long, people were commenting to the proud Hattie Mae, "That child is gifted."[12]

Hattie Mae Lee's strong personality and determined spirit had a long-lasting impact on Oprah Winfrey. Because of her strict discipline and rules, her stress on education, and her strong faith in God, these traits became deeply rooted in the young girl. Even when everything else about Oprah's life changed, Hattie Mae's lessons remain the fundamental principles that she lives by today. Winfrey is grateful for her grandmother's efforts in raising her. She has said that her grandmother instilled a kind of strength and a belief system in her that have remained with her always.[13]

When she was six years old, Oprah's life took a dramatic turn. Her mother, Vernita Lee, living in Milwaukee and working as a maid, was ready for her daughter to join her. Oprah left the tranquil countryside of Mississippi and headed north.

3

DANGEROUS TIMES

 ix-year-old Oprah Winfrey began life with her mother in downtown Milwaukee. Living in a big city was quite a change for her. She had been used to the warm weather and open spaces of the Mississippi countryside. Instead, she now found herself surrounded by tall buildings and busy streets. Concrete pavement replaced the soft earth of the Mississippi countryside. Being in the northern part of the United States also meant that Oprah would see snow regularly each winter. No longer could she run barefoot during much of the year as she had on the farm with Hattie Mae.

Oprah and her mother lived in a single room in a boardinghouse on Ninth Street. To make things even more difficult, Vernita had another baby by this time, named Patricia. Oprah was now confronted with the irritation of having to share her mother's attention with a sibling. In addition, Vernita worked long hours every day to support her family. Not having a car, she went to and from her job by bus. She left early each morning and came home late each night. That, along with the attention the baby required, left Oprah feeling lonely and neglected. Years later, Oprah would

When Oprah was six, she moved from her grandmother's country home to live with her mother in the crowded city of Milwaukee.

understand her mother's situation better. But at the time, it was hard.

As she settled into her new life in Milwaukee, Oprah would find public speaking to be an outlet for her, just as it had been in Kosciusko. As she later recalled, "From the time I was eight years old, I was a champion speaker. I spoke for every women's group, banquet, church function—I did the circuit. Anybody needed anybody to speak anything, they'd call me."[1]

One great thing about life with her mother was that she had a television set. Oprah loved watching it, especially her favorite shows, *I Love Lucy* and *Leave It to Beaver*.

After a year, things were not working out as well as Vernita had planned for her little family. Oprah was unhappy with her life there. She needed more attention than Vernita could give. Looking for a solution, Vernita called Oprah's father, Vernon, to see whether he would let Oprah come live with him.

By this time, Vernon Winfrey was out of the Army and settled in Nashville, Tennessee. He had built a stable life for himself and his wife, Zelma, in a small house on the east side of the city. To earn a living, Vernon worked two jobs—cleaning floors at Vanderbilt University and scrubbing pots at a hospital.

Vernon and Zelma were delighted with the idea of having Oprah come live with them. They had been unable to have a child of their own, and Oprah would be a welcome addition to their household. So Oprah made the move from Milwaukee to Nashville. Once again she was faced with adapting to a brand-new lifestyle and set of rules. Unlike Vernita Lee, Vernon and Zelma Winfrey were strict parents. From the start, Oprah was expected to make her bed, wash dishes, and keep her room clean.

The Winfreys were also concerned about Oprah's education. When they found out she would be starting third grade after skipping second grade in Milwaukee, they wanted to make sure she would be ready. Zelma spent the summer drilling Oprah on her multiplication tables and helping her get prepared for school. Vernon left a page of addition and subtraction problems for her to solve each day, too.

Vernon and Zelma Winfrey's strict rules were rigid and demanding. Yet along with their discipline came the attention and encouragement Oprah had needed for so long. They gave Oprah a stable, caring home and lifestyle. Soon she felt comfortable and secure.

At the end of her first year in Nashville, Vernon and Zelma sent Oprah back to Milwaukee for a summer visit with her mother. By that time, Vernita had moved into a two-bedroom apartment. She also had a new baby, a boy named Jeffrey.

It was not long before Vernita Lee decided she wanted Oprah to move back in with her again. She thought the earlier problems had been solved. She also planned to get married and then move into a house with her new husband. With Oprah back, she would have all her children with her, and they could be a real family.

When the summer vacation was over and Vernon Winfrey went to Milwaukee to bring Oprah back to Nashville with him, Vernita refused to let her go. Vernon sadly returned to Nashville without his daughter.

In Milwaukee the old problems returned, as far as Oprah was concerned. Vernita's marriage hopes never worked out, so the family stayed in their cramped two-bedroom apartment. Instead of a room of her own as she had in Nashville, Oprah was sharing a bedroom with Patricia and Jeffrey. Now she had two siblings to compete with for attention.

Soon after she moved back with her mother, Oprah's life in Milwaukee became even more difficult. Only nine years old, she was raped one night by a nineteen-year-old cousin who was taking care of her. Not knowing what to do, she kept the incident secret for years. As she later recalled, "I was a child who did not tell, because I did not feel that I would have been validated."[2]

But that was not all. Over the next several years she would continue to suffer sexual abuse from another relative and a family friend. Oprah's life had quickly become confusing and frightening. She lived in constant fear that she would become pregnant. She later said, "Every time I had a stomachache, I thought I was pregnant. . . . That for me was the terror. . . ."[3] She also remembers blaming herself for the abuse, and thinking that something must be wrong with her.[4]

Oprah went on with her life, all the while keeping her secret. At school, even though she was younger than her classmates, her schoolwork excelled. She began to feel the pleasure and power that came from doing well in school. As a good student, she could get the attention and praise from her teachers that she was unable to get at home.[5] Yet her academic success often alienated her from her classmates. For the next six years, she would have few school friends. She learned to withdraw into her own world by reading.

When Oprah was thirteen, she began attending Lincoln Middle School in downtown Milwaukee. One of her teachers, Gene Abrams, noticed her reading by herself in the cafeteria during lunch. Realizing her potential as well as her loneliness, he wanted to help. Abrams recommended Oprah for a new program called Upward Bound. It was 1967, and some schools were promoting programs that would help spur inter-racial understanding. The purpose of Upward Bound was to bring minorities, especially African Americans, into affluent white schools. There they could take advantage of more academic opportunities. By being in classes together, black and white students could also get to know one another and have a chance to become friends.

Through Abrams's efforts, Oprah received a full scholarship to Nicolet High School. When she began eighth grade there, she was the only African American among the two thousand students. Unlike her earlier school experiences, at Nicolet many students were friendly to Oprah, partly because she was African American. Many of her classmates wanted to get to know her because she was different.

For Oprah, going to Nicolet High School turned out to be a mixed experience. She was exposed to a different world from the one she was used to at Lincoln. All at once she was in a place of privilege, where students had every advantage and opportunity. Still, that very exposure left her feeling confused and unhappy. For the first time in her life, she realized that she was poor. As Oprah later explained, "As long as no one tells you otherwise and you don't see the other side, you're okay. But in that new school I felt unimportant and insecure."[6]

Nicolet was in Glendale, Wisconsin, twenty miles from her home in downtown Milwaukee. Oprah had to ride three different buses to get there each day. She commuted from the inner city to the suburbs along with maids like her mother. It made her feel lonely, poor, and different. She soon realized that her friends at Nicolet were living lives like those she saw on *Leave*

Winfrey received a full scholarship to Nicolet High School in Milwaukee. She was the only African American among the two thousand students at the school.

It to Beaver and other television shows. She wanted her mother to be like their mothers. She wanted to have cookies waiting for her when she got home from school.[7] Instead, she had to go home every afternoon to the poverty, noise, and danger of the inner city.

Oprah's lack of parental guidance and her ongoing sexual abuse combined to make her not only unhappy and confused but angry and rebellious as well. Her behavior began to show it. She stole money from her mother's purse. She stayed out late at night and told lies. Once, she staged a robbery in her apartment in an attempt to persuade her mother to let her keep a puppy as a guard dog. Another time, she broke her eyeglasses on purpose so that her mother would have to buy her a new pair.

By the time Oprah was fourteen, Vernita Lee had had enough of her daughter's difficult behavior. She realized that she was not able to care for Oprah in the way she needed. In desperation, she decided to put Oprah in a home for delinquent girls. When she went to apply, she was told that the home was full and that she should try again in a few weeks. Not wanting to wait, Vernita Lee turned once again to Vernon Winfrey in Nashville.

4

"THE GRAND OLE OPRAH"

ashville, another big city, is about the same size as Milwaukee. Located in central Tennessee, Nashville is the center of country music—the home of the Grand Ole Opry. Nashville is also the capital of Tennessee and is known for its elegant Greek Revival architecture. The city is sometimes called "the Athens of the South."

By this time Vernon had opened a neighborhood barbershop and general store just a few blocks from the Winfrey home. He and Zelma were glad to get Oprah settled with them again in their little brick house. Vernon had felt all along that he and his wife were able to provide a better environment in which to raise his daughter. Oprah could start a new life there and leave behind the troubles of the past.

After only a few weeks in Nashville, it became evident that Oprah's past would not fade so easily. Fourteen-year-old Oprah was pregnant. She was terrified to tell her father, and she hid her condition for as long as she could.[1] On the day she told him, the baby was born prematurely and died shortly afterward. Winfrey later described this time in her life as "my greatest shame."[2]

Oprah had changed a lot from the nine-year-old that Vernon and Zelma had known before. During her past five years in Milwaukee, Oprah's manners had disappeared. Now she had an attitude. Vernon was shocked to hear her call him "Pops." She also wore heavy makeup and clothes the Winfreys found alarming. Her skirts were too short and tight, and she wore halter tops that they considered too revealing for a girl her age.

Vernon set down the rules with Oprah from the start. He told her, "You will not live in this house unless you abide by my rules."[3] No more calling him "Pops"; she would speak to her father with respect. He expected good manners and to be obeyed without question. The Winfreys also overhauled Oprah's appearance. They made sure she dressed in clothes that were more conservative, and they allowed her to wear just a little makeup.

Vernon and Zelma did not stop with Oprah's appearance and manners. They renewed their emphasis on her education as well. First, they expected her to learn five new vocabulary words each day. She could choose the words, but she had to spell them correctly and show that she could use them in sentences. Otherwise, she went without her dinner that night. Zelma also took Oprah to the library every two weeks, where she chose five books to read. Not only did the Winfreys require her to read the books, but she had to write reports about them, too.

By the time she was fourteen, Oprah was a wild teenager in need of a fresh start in life. She went to live with her father, Vernon Winfrey, and his wife, Zelma, in this small brick home in Nashville, Tennessee.

With all that and schoolwork, too, Oprah did not have as much time for television as she had at Vernita's. In fact, Vernon and Zelma made sure of that by limiting her television viewing to just one hour each day. And she had to finish her schoolwork first. By the time Oprah was ready to watch television each evening, the nightly news was on. So that was what she often watched. Her permissive life with Vernita had been turned upside down. Later, describing life with Vernon, Winfrey said, "I could not get away with anything because when my father said something, he absolutely meant it."[4]

With so many rules, you might think that Oprah would have hated living with the Winfreys. But somewhere deep within her she adjusted and began to thrive. Slowly, with the structure and discipline of her new lifestyle, Oprah's life began to change. "I went back to school after the baby died, thinking that I had been given a second chance in my life."[5]

In the fall of 1968, Oprah began the tenth grade at Nashville's East High School. She soon found that East High School was different from the two schools she had attended in Milwaukee. Unlike Nicolet, East had students who were mainly from middle-class families like the Winfreys. She was one of many African-American students enrolled there. And unlike Lincoln, East High School had enough books and supplies for its students.

Still, because of all the changes and upheavals in her life, Oprah's first grades were disappointing—mainly C's. While that might have been all right with her mother, Vernon thought differently. He knew Oprah could do much better, and he expected nothing but her best. Vernon told her, "If you were a child who could only get C's, then that is all I would expect of you. But you are not. So in this house, C's are not acceptable."[6]

Oprah knew her father was serious, so she began working harder. She became an honor-roll student for the remainder of her high school days. According to her tenth-grade English teacher, Oprah was a "wonderful student" and an "excellent speaker."[7] She also became active in student organizations, choosing clubs that would allow her to build on her speaking and acting skills.

During her high school years, Oprah continued giving dramatic readings for church and civic groups. Vernon Winfrey was active in the Faith Missionary Baptist Church, and he made sure his daughter attended services regularly as well. At the same time, Oprah began to learn more about her heritage as an African American. Through the words of Harriet Tubman, abolitionist Sojourner Truth, and poet Margaret Walker, she discovered the courage and dignity of others. These African-American women, along with writer Maya Angelou, became her heroes. When she was sixteen, Oprah used her talent in speech and drama to win a national contest sponsored by the Elks Club. The prize was a full scholarship—four years' tuition·to the university of her choice.

As her life at East High School continued, Oprah found to her delight that she fit in. Not only did she excel at her schoolwork, but her popularity with the other students exploded for the first time in her life. In other newly integrated schools, a sense of fear and distrust often plagued relationships between black and white students, but not for Oprah Winfrey. By her seventeenth birthday, Oprah had so many friends that she held her birthday party in the school gym and invited the entire student body.

During her senior year, Oprah was elected vice president of the Student Council. She won with the slogan "Vote for the Grand Ole Oprah," showing her ever-present sense of humor and creativity. She was also chosen to attend the White House Conference on Youth in Estes Park, Colorado. She was picked because of her grades, leadership skills, and community ser-vice. To cap her accomplishments, she was elected "Most Popular Girl" during her senior year. At the same time, her boyfriend, Anthony Otey, was named "Most Popular Boy."

While in high school, Oprah was also involved in projects to help others. During her senior year, one such project was a March of Dimes walkathon. Oprah

Oprah's 1969 yearbook photo from East High School in Nashville:
Oprah did well in school there and was so popular that she held her
seventeenth birthday party in the gym and invited the whole school.

began enlisting sponsors to donate money for each mile she walked in the walkathon. The farther she walked, the more money she would raise for the March of Dimes. One of Oprah's sponsors was the Nashville radio station WVOL. When she returned to collect WVOL's donation after the walkathon, she spoke with the station's producer, John Heidelberg. He was impressed with her voice and personality, and he suggested that she read into a microphone just for fun. Oprah read some news, and Heidelberg made a demonstration tape.

At that moment, all her years of dramatic readings paid off. Oprah's confidence, along with the natural richness and warmth of her voice, were perfect for broadcasting. Delighted with her ability, WVOL hired Oprah as a part-time announcer. She read the news on WVOL after school and on weekends. After a brief training period, she began earning $100 each week.

Besides giving her an impressive income for a teenager, working at WVOL also broadened Oprah's view of the world. Through her job, she became immersed in the current events of Nashville and the world. Equally important, she was able to build her confidence and learn firsthand how to function as a professional in a place of work.

Each year the Nashville fire department sponsored a beauty contest to choose Miss Fire Prevention for the city. The winning contestant's job was to promote fire safety during her reigning year. Local businesses often chose one of their employees to participate in the contest.

Up until this time, the women who won Miss Fire Prevention had always been white. Sometimes the winners even had flaming red hair, emphasizing the theme of the title. Nevertheless, in 1971 WVOL decided to enter Winfrey to represent the station in the pageant. As the event proceeded, Winfrey became one of three finalists. The tension mounted as the judges decided who would win. As a final question, each contestant was asked, "What would you do if you had one million dollars?"

The first two finalists answered predictably. One said she would use the money to help her family. The second said she would help the poor. But when Winfrey's turn came, her answer surprised everyone. She grinned and said, "If I had a million dollars, I'd be a spending fool!"[8] The judges were delighted with her originality and personality, and Winfrey became Nashville's first African-American Miss Fire Prevention that October day.

In 1971, Winfrey used her Elks Club scholarship and began her freshman year at Tennessee State University. This all-black university in Nashville was known for its solid programs in speech and drama, the area Winfrey chose as her major.

Although Winfrey had wanted to attend college in

In 1971, Oprah Winfrey entered a beauty contest for Nashville's Miss Fire Prevention. She impressed the judges and became the first African American to win the title.

another city so she could live on her own, money was tight in the Winfrey household. Living away from home would be expensive for a full-time college student. Since Tennessee State University was only about seven miles from her house, she could live at home. By staying in Nashville, she could also continue her work at WVOL.

After such a successful high school experience, Winfrey's college years were disappointing. As she began college, the American civil rights movement was well under way. Yet by this time, many African Americans had become increasingly dissatisfied with the slow pace of progress toward equal rights. The Black Power movement, which promoted change through violence, had gained strength. Many young African Americans were angrily protesting their unequal treatment for jobs and other opportunities. Their anger sometimes exploded in violence and destruction. As Winfrey remembers that time: "Everybody was angry for four years. [Tennessee State University] was an all-black college and it was in to be angry."[9]

Winfrey's problem was that she did not feel the anger of other African Americans her age. Her high school experience in Nashville had been extremely positive. Other blacks had felt the humiliation of treatment as "second-class citizens," but from Winfrey's perspective, hard work had brought her success, regardless of her color. She wanted to use her time working and getting her education rather than protesting. But by not fitting in, Winfrey has said, she felt resentment from the more militant students. As a result, she hated her college years.[10]

As a distraction from her schoolwork, Winfrey continued to enter beauty contests. Despite her participation, she never thought of herself as a beauty. Speaking about her appearance, Winfrey has said, "The word 'beautiful' isn't even in my vocabulary."[11] So when she won the titles of both Miss Black Nashville and Miss Black Tennessee in 1972, she was quite surprised. With honesty and humor, she has explained, "I did not expect to win, nor did anybody else expect me to. . . . And Lord, were they [the other contestants] upset, and I was upset for them, really, I was. I said, 'Beats me, girls, I'm as shocked as you are.'"[12]

Reflecting on her success in beauty pageants, Winfrey is realistic and down to earth. She says, "I had marvelous poise and talent and could handle any question, and I would always win on the talent part, which was usually a dramatic reading. I could—I still can—hold my own easily."[13] Winfrey also entered the Miss Black America contest that year, held in Hollywood, California. Although she did not win that title, the experience she gained in maintaining her confidence and poise under pressure would later help her as she began to build her career.

With so much hometown attention on Winfrey, a Nashville television station, WTVF, asked her to audition for the job of coanchor for the six o'clock evening news. By this time, in order to gain equal treatment for people regardless of race or sex, the government had developed a set of guidelines for businesses to follow. These guidelines were broadly referred to as "affirmative action." They were put into place to help minorities, especially African Americans and women, get good jobs. With affirmative action, businesses were encouraged to hire minorities, in an effort to help them catch up from years of discrimination and unfair treatment.

At that time there were no African-American newscasters in Nashville. WTVF recognized Winfrey's talent, but management also realized that by hiring her the station would be complying with the government's affirmative action guidelines. In addition, management thought an African-American woman coanchor might be especially popular with the minorities in the viewing audience.

Winfrey knew this job would be a wonderful opportunity to begin building her career. Listening to her audition tape, WTVF managers were impressed with her as well. She had the look, the warmth, and the air of authority they wanted. With that, Winfrey became the first African American and the youngest woman to coanchor television news in Nashville. She was still a college student and was now also earning $15,000 a year.

Although Winfrey was hired to do the weekend news, she was soon promoted to do the evening news every weeknight. Her coanchor was Harry Chapman. Together they reviewed the day's stories and decided who would cover which news items each evening. Chris Clark, the news director at WTVF, became Winfrey's trusted boss and mentor.

After four years of study at Tennessee State University and working at WTVF, things were going well for Winfrey. Yet her restlessness at home had only increased. Still living with Vernon, Zelma, and all Vernon's rules, she felt ready for more independence.

When another television station, WJZ-TV in Baltimore, Maryland, contacted her about a job, Winfrey was interested. Although she would not have time to complete her senior project—and so would not receive her college degree—working for WJZ-TV would mean a better contract and more money in a bigger city. It would also mean that she could be on her own for the first time. When they offered her a position as news coanchor, she accepted. As she headed east to Baltimore in June 1976, Oprah Winfrey's future looked bright.

5

A Change in Plans

n 1976 Baltimore was the tenth-largest city in the country. Located on the eastern seaboard, it is an old city, dating back to 1729. Baltimore has an aura of history, East Coast sophistication, and southern charm.

WJZ-TV welcomed Oprah Winfrey's arrival in Baltimore with a citywide campaign to spark viewers' interest. Promoting her unusual name, "What's an Oprah?" bellowed from billboards throughout the city. Everyone would find out on her first broadcast, scheduled for August 16.

In the meantime, Winfrey stretched her wings with

her newfound independence. Finally she was alone in
a new city without Vernon to restrict her behavior. She
found her first apartment and settled into her new
surroundings during the summer.

As in Nashville, Winfrey was hired to coanchor the
six o'clock evening news. Her partner, Jerry Turner, was
one of the most popular news anchors in the city.
Turner's appearance was in stark contrast to Winfrey's.
He was a tall, slender, white male with silver hair and a
calm, charming style. Oprah Winfrey was only twenty-
two years old then and completely unknown to
Baltimore citizens. Both coanchors, however, were
competitive and ambitious.

On August 16, 1976, Winfrey appeared on the six
o'clock evening news in Baltimore for the first time.
Sporting a short, perfectly round Afro hairstyle and
wearing a red jacket with a wide Peter Pan collar,
Winfrey looked every bit the bright and eager news
professional. Yet it soon became apparent, despite all
the advertising and high hopes, that her new position
was not going to work out as expected. Winfrey's style
of reporting the news had worked well for her in
Nashville. There, she had come across as warm and
genuine. Nashville viewers had seen her style as a
refreshing change from the more formal approach of
most of their other television reporters.

Baltimore viewers were different. They were used to
a more polished, professional performance from their

newscasters. They did not expect to see spontaneity or emotion in their evening news. Winfrey's emotions and out-front style kept getting in her way. When she reported tragic stories—and many of them were—the viewers could tell she was upset. Once, when talking about a house fire in which seven children were killed, Winfrey actually cried during the report.

There were other problems as well. Winfrey mispronounced words on occasion. One evening she mispronounced the word *Canada* three times in the same broadcast. She even giggled once to hide her embarrassment.

Winfrey also did not read her stories straight from the script on the TelePrompTer, as she was supposed to. She liked to ad-lib when she thought she could improve the story and come across to viewers as more natural. After all, this approach had worked for her in Nashville. But the station managers in Baltimore did not see it that way. They wanted her to read the news word by word and leave nothing to chance.

Winfrey and coanchor Turner were at odds. Their partnership became more like a rivalry, with Winfrey's inexperience putting her at a disadvantage against Turner's polish. With all these problems, Winfrey lost her job as coanchor of WJZ-TV on April 1, 1977. As she said later, "I had no business anchoring the news in a major market."[1] Yet Winfrey had been used to succeeding at everything she attempted. This was the first time she had ever tried something new, worked hard at it, and failed.

After that, things got even worse. The station was unable to recognize and use Winfrey's strengths. Instead, they decided she needed to change, and her makeover began. First, the station manager sent her to a famous dressmaker to improve her wardrobe. Then he sent her to a French beauty salon in New York to redo her hairstyle. The only problem was that the salon treatment caused Winfrey's hair to fall out within a week—every bit of it! To make matters worse, she could not find a wig that would fit her head. She had to wear scarves until her hair finally grew back. Winfrey was mortified. She cried constantly and her self-confidence plummeted.[2]

WJZ-TV was not finished with her yet. Next they sent her to a voice coach to work on improving the way she spoke. Luckily, the voice coach realized that there was nothing wrong with Winfrey's voice at all. The only thing wrong was that Winfrey was letting the station try to change her. Her voice coach told her to go back to the station and stand up for herself. She should not let them try to change her anymore.

Looking back, Winfrey felt that her voice coach's advice was particularly helpful. All she needed to succeed was a job that was right for her—a job that would take advantage of her natural abilities. That chance finally came when WJZ-TV made Winfrey a cohost of its new talk show, *People Are Talking*. The new assignment worked for the station, and it worked for Winfrey. The show's format allowed her warmth, charisma, and enthusiasm to shine through. Winfrey said later that "they didn't know what to do with me. And that's really how I ended up doing a talk show."[3]

By the time Winfrey began cohosting *People Are Talking*, talk shows had been on the air for many years. Once television viewing exploded after World War II, one of the earliest television talk shows was the *Today Show*, hosted by Dave Garroway and his chimpanzee sidekick, J. Fred Muggs.

Over the years, talk show hosts Merv Griffin, Jack Paar, Johnny Carson, and others had featured a celebrity-interview format with a variety of guests who wanted to promote their latest books, movies, television shows, or political beliefs. With *People Are Talking*, Oprah Winfrey contributed to a new age of talk shows in which local chatter and personal, often tragic, stories were featured.

Today, this type of talk show can be seen on television during all hours of the day and night. Because they are inexpensive to produce and can draw huge audiences, the successful shows are very profitable. A talk show's popularity depends on the host and his or her ability to keep the viewers interested. Although being a talk show host may look easy and many people have tried it, many have also failed.

Along with Winfrey, Richard Sher cohosted the new Baltimore talk show. From the beginning, Winfrey and Sher worked well together. Winfrey quickly realized that she had found the right job. After beginning her work on *People Are Talking*, she said, "The minute the first show was over I thought, 'Thank God, I've found what I was meant to do.' It's like breathing to me."[4]

The station knew it, too. Even though *People Are Talking* was aired at the same time as the wildly popular *Donahue Show*, Winfrey's audience began to grow. Before long, *People Are Talking* was beating *The Donahue Show* in the local television ratings.

One key to Winfrey's success was her naturalness with her audience and her guests. As she has said, "I go on the air every day, and it's like having a conversation with whoever the guest is."[5] Because of that, she used no script during the show. That allowed her to ask questions and change direction to keep the show moving and interesting. All her experiences performing in front of large groups as she was growing up had given her the confidence and poise to be comfortable in front of an audience. And on top of it all, she had fun.

Winfrey also became known for her ability to empathize with her guests and her audiences. One reason for that was all the difficulties she had faced in her early years. She knew what it was like to be poor, to move to a strange place, to live in the inner city, to be

"They didn't know what to do with me. And that's really how I ended up doing a talk show," said Winfrey about her first talk show, *People Are Talking*, on a local Baltimore station.

sexually abused. She understood loneliness and pain. She even knew what it was like to turn to destructive behavior for attention. As she later explained, "I'm every woman. I make no judgments. I allow my vulnerability to show through. People recognize when you are willing to be raw and truthful, and it's a relief to have somebody not try to be perfect. They see themselves in me."[6]

Winfrey's natural friendliness and sincere interest in other people and their stories also contributed to her success. Most people like to talk about themselves if they think their listener cares and will understand

Oprah Winfrey says that for her, hosting a talk show feels as natural as breathing. "It is what I was meant to do."

their point of view. Winfrey is able to convey that understanding immediately to her guests; most people find it easy to open up to her. They also respond to her intelligence and quick wit. She is able to keep the interviews lively and interesting for her guests and for her audience.

Nevertheless, no life is ever entirely perfect for long. That is also true for Oprah Winfrey. Off camera, away from her newfound success at the studios of WJZ-TV, she began eating more and gaining weight. Oprah has said that eating became a way of cushioning herself against the problems and anxiety in her life.[7]

She also became entangled in several unhappy relationships with men who did not treat her well. Once, when one of those relationships ended, she became so depressed that she even considered suicide. Ultimately, though, Winfrey's spirit rose to defy her depression. She decided then that she would never let anyone have that much power over her again.[8]

During her time in Baltimore, Winfrey expanded her activities outside work as well. She became involved in the community by visiting schools, speaking in churches, and making appearances as a local celebrity for civic groups. Often her focus was on helping children. She encouraged them to read and to learn to express themselves well. After all, those were two of the things that had been so helpful to her own success.

After six years with *People Are Talking*, Winfrey decided it was time to move on. Ever ambitious, she was ready for a bigger challenge. She also wanted the chance to host a talk show by herself. She just could not decide where she wanted to go.

In 1983, Debra DiMaio, one of the producers of *People Are Talking*, was also looking for a bigger challenge. After showing a tape of the show to the managers of WLS-TV in Chicago, DiMaio was hired to produce their morning talk show, *A.M. Chicago*. As it happened, *A.M. Chicago* also needed a new host. Their former host, Rob Weller, had recently left for another opportunity.

By 1983, Winfrey's life in Baltimore was a success. Through hard work, talent, and luck, she had an interesting job at which she excelled. Her future was soon to become brighter than she could have ever imagined.

6

BLAST OFF IN CHICAGO

he talk show *A.M. Chicago* had been on the air since 1974. Designed to air local news and provide guest appearances from local celebrities and soap-opera stars, it was shown on Chicago's ABC-affiliated television station after *Good Morning, America*. When Debra DiMaio joined the staff of *A.M. Chicago*, the show had dismal ratings. It was the third-ranking morning show in the Chicago television viewing area. One big problem was that it was competing against the number-one talk show in the nation, *The Donahue Show*.

Hosted by Phil Donahue, *The Donahue Show* began

in 1967 in Dayton, Ohio. Since 1974, Chicago had been its home, and it was seen on WGN-TV. It had quickly become extremely popular with audiences across the nation. It was Donahue who began the practice of going out into the audience with a handheld microphone, inviting the audience to participate in the show by asking the guests questions and giving feedback. That practice proved very effective and is commonly used by talk show hosts today.

By 1984, Phil Donahue had been hosting the nation's most popular daytime talk show for sixteen years. With his snow-white hair and handsome good looks, Donahue was adored by housewives everywhere. He had a mature, confident style that they were eager to see every morning. He had also built a reputation for having more intellectual, thought-provoking content than most other talk shows.

When Dennis Swanson, the WLS-TV vice president and general sales manager, was desperately searching for a new host for the failing *A.M. Chicago*, his new producer, Debra DiMaio, suggested Winfrey. Swanson was immediately impressed when he learned that *People Are Talking* was beating *The Donahue Show* in the local Baltimore ratings. Reviewing DiMaio's tape of *People Are Talking* once again, Swanson thought Winfrey might indeed be right for the job.

Oprah Winfrey was not so sure. Yes, she was ready for a new challenge in a larger city with a larger

At the time Oprah Winfrey began her talk show career, the most
popular talk show in the nation was *The Donahue Show*. Host Phil
Donahue was the first to take a microphone into the audience and
invite the guests to ask questions and make comments.

viewing audience. Chicago would fill that need, having the country's third-largest television-viewing audience. But Chicago also had a reputation for being a particularly racist city. As an African-American woman, how could she possibly do well there? She would be up against Donahue—and in his hometown, at that! Winfrey was apprehensive when she flew to Chicago to interview with Swanson over Labor Day in 1983.

After meeting her, Swanson was convinced that Winfrey would be right for the show. He saw her warmth, sincerity, and enthusiasm as different from what other talk show hosts had to offer. Where Donahue was intellectual, Winfrey was emotional. Where Donahue was analytical, Winfrey was empathetic. Even Winfrey said, "He'd [Donahue] do nuclear disarmament much better than I would. He'd have all the stats, be very thorough, and I'd be accused of being overemotional."[1] Swanson thought that the viewing audience would respond to her. He said, "I think you have a gift and I'd like you to share it with this television station."[2]

For Winfrey's part, she was drawn by the challenge that would await her if she accepted the job. Competitive by nature, would she be able to improve *A.M. Chicago*'s ratings? She wanted to find out. At twenty-nine years old, Winfrey signed a four-year contract with WLS. She would be making $200,000 each of those years hosting *A.M. Chicago*.

🔲🔳🔲🔳🔲🔳🔲🔳🔲🔳🔲🔳🔲🔳🔲🔳🔲🔳🔲🔳🔲🔳🔲🔳🔲🔳🔲🔳

According to Debra DiMaio, "It was a bold move to hire a black female to host a talk show in a city so racially polarized."[3] Dennis Swanson said, "She was the best, and I wanted the best."[4]

When the managers at WJZ-TV heard of Winfrey's Chicago offer, they tried to convince her to stay in Baltimore. How things had changed since her dismal beginning there in 1976! But the station could not compete with the salary and opportunity that WLS offered her. With a tinge of sadness in her heart at leaving her friends in Baltimore, Winfrey looked to her future in Chicago.

Chicago is one of the largest cities in the United States. It spreads west from the shores of Lake Michigan in northern Illinois. Chicago is known as "the Windy City" because of the fierce winds that continually blow off Lake Michigan. Its weather is much like the weather Winfrey knew as a girl in Milwaukee. The summers are hot and humid, but the winters are brutally cold, with bone-chilling winds and lots of snow and ice.

Despite her experience and self-confidence, Winfrey was a bundle of nerves as she got ready for her first *A.M. Chicago* show. It would be broadcast at 9:00 A.M. on January 2, 1984—head-to-head against *The Donahue Show*.

As she began preparing for that first show, Winfrey also analyzed her viewing audience. She knew she would be competing with *The Donahue Show* for the same viewers. Most would be white, middle-class, stay-at-home moms. On the surface, their lives were very different from hers. But underneath those differences lay a common thread. Winfrey knew that deep down, regardless of race, status, or background, most people want the same basic things. They want to be happy and to be loved. She has said, "One of my greatest assets is knowing I'm no different from the viewer."[5] Winfrey would build her show on that common ground.

Once again, Winfrey's down-to-earth style immediately swept her to the height of popularity. Like Phil Donahue, she used a handheld microphone and mingled with her studio audience during the show. Guests were able to see firsthand the Winfrey charisma that has made her one of the most popular women in America.[6]

Her Chicago viewers also discovered that Winfrey was someone they could relate to. Sometimes during the show she would kick off her shoes and complain that her feet hurt. Her audience could certainly understand that. Her viewers also began to see Winfrey laugh and cry right along with her guests in the style that would soon become familiar to millions. The same emotions that had gotten her into trouble as a newscaster were helping her establish a rapport and popularity with her viewers. As she assessed her appeal in an interview, Winfrey later said, "When people

Winfrey is naturally friendly and interested in others. She is not afraid to show her emotions—to laugh and cry along with her guests.

watch television, they are looking to see themselves. I think the reason why I work as well as I do on the air is that people sense the realness."[7]

Before Winfrey, most of *A.M. Chicago*'s guests had been soap-opera stars. But Winfrey began to change the scope of the show, choosing to interview big-name celebrities instead. Her guests included such stars as Stevie Wonder, Shirley MacLaine, Tom Selleck, Christie Brinkley, Dudley Moore, Candace Bergen, and Billy Dee Williams. She also wanted the show's content to be more challenging, just as *The Donahue Show* was. She used some shows to explore difficult and controversial life issues such as incest, child abuse, and eating disorders.

Over time, she also began sharing parts of herself and her life. Because she was sincerely interested in her guests and her audiences, she could expose her issues with men, weight, and child abuse. Once again, people could relate to her as a real human being, with real feelings and vulnerability. She felt that because of the different kinds of experiences she had as a child, she was better able to understand the experiences of others.[8] According to another talk show host, Maury Povich, "The closest thing that Phil Donahue ever talked about was the fact that he was a wayward Catholic. Other than that, talk-show hosts did not talk about themselves."[9] This, more than anything else, began to endear Winfrey to her audiences. It also began to separate her from her competition.

From the start, Winfrey was a hit on *A.M. Chicago*. In just four weeks, she took the show from last place to first place in its time slot. Suddenly, *The Donahue Show* had been knocked down to second place.

After seven months, Swanson decided to build on *A.M. Chicago*'s newfound success. He expanded the show from its thirty-minute format to a full hour. Before long, Winfrey began to draw national attention. By December 1984, Winfrey had caught the eye of *Newsweek* magazine, which described her as "Chicago's hottest media star."[10]

7

THE COLOR OF SUCCESS

n her thirty-first birthday, a nervous Oprah Winfrey was introduced to the nation for the first time. She was a guest on *The Tonight Show*, one of the country's most popular late-night talk shows. Johnny Carson, the host, was known for promoting new celebrities, and her appearance on the show was a great opportunity for Winfrey. She could make more people aware of who she was and her success on *A.M. Chicago*.

That night, by chance, Quincy Jones, the well-known composer and record producer, was also one of Carson's guests. Winfrey did not know it yet, but their meeting would soon prove to be important for them both.

Several months later Winfrey and Jones met again, but under quite different circumstances. Jones was in Chicago on business for only a few hours. While there, he turned on the television set in his hotel room and happened to catch *A.M. Chicago* in progress. As he watched Oprah Winfrey, an idea began to form in Jones's mind. He thought Winfrey might be perfect for a part in a new movie he was working on with Steven Spielberg. Would she have any interest in auditioning?

The movie Jones had in mind was *The Color Purple*. It was based on a novel by Alice Walker that had won the Pulitzer Prize for fiction in 1983. The movie's director, Steven Spielberg, was well known for his many blockbuster movies, such as *E.T.*, *Raiders of the Lost Ark*, and *Jaws*. *The Color Purple* would be Spielberg's first movie about a serious subject. As a composer, Jones was writing the music for the film. He was coproducing it as well.

The Color Purple is about a poor African-American girl named Celie and her life growing up in the South in the early 1900s. It is a story of quiet courage and hope in the midst of abuse, discrimination, and poverty. In the movie, actress Whoopi Goldberg would play Celie. Sofia, Celie's strong-minded daughter-in-law, is another important character in the story. Watching

Winfrey that morning on television, Jones thought she might be just the right person to play the role of Sofia.[1]

What Jones would soon find out was that *The Color Purple* was one of Winfrey's favorite books. When it was published in 1982, Oprah had read it and loved it. She later said, "I remember . . . going up to the mall and buying every single copy that they had in stock. I read it that day. I was devastated, overwhelmed, empowered."[2] She liked it so much that she gave copies of the book to all her friends. According to Winfrey, "When I heard they were going to make a movie of it, I thought, 'Oh, Lord, I will do anything to be involved—anything!'"[3] When Jones called her that day and asked if she would like to audition for the part of Sofia, Winfrey was elated.

Without ever having taken a single acting lesson, Winfrey auditioned for the part—and got it. Still, with all her excitement, she also felt fearful: What if she did her best and it still was not good enough?[4]

Winfrey threw herself into preparing for her acting debut. She used civil rights worker Fannie Lou Hamer as her role model for the part. In addition, Winfrey's knowledge of the courageous African-American women she had highlighted in so many speeches as a teenager found a voice in Sofia. Winfrey said, "[Sofia] was part of all those women I'd been carrying around inside me for years."[5] In the movie, Sofia has a hard life and suffers abuse and mistreatment. But through her core of faith in herself, she recovers and takes control of her life. Sofia was exactly the kind of woman Winfrey loved and respected.

The movie was filmed in Monroe, North Carolina. Winfrey would have to take a leave of absence from *A.M. Chicago* for three months. During that time, the show continued by using guest hosts and showing reruns.

The Color Purple was released to the public in December 1985. Reviews of the film were mixed, but Winfrey's acting was praised. *Newsweek*'s favorable review called Winfrey "a brazen delight" in her portrayal of Sofia.[6] The movie also gave more and more people across the nation an introduction to this rising celebrity.

One of the many people to see *The Color Purple* was Vernon Winfrey. Back in Nashville, he did not want to miss his daughter's performance. It was the first movie he had seen in twenty-five years.

When the time came for the annual Academy Awards ceremony to honor the best in films for 1985, *The Color Purple* received eleven nominations. Even though this was Winfrey's very first acting role, she received an Academy Award nomination for Best Actress in a Supporting Role.

To prepare for her appearance at the Academy Award presentation in spring 1986, Winfrey wore a spectacular ivory and gold gown trimmed in beads.

She also wore a diamond necklace and earrings. The only problem was that the dress had been altered right before the event. To her horror, she discovered as she was dressing to go to the ceremony that the dress was too tight. In fact, it was so tight she could hardly sit down in it and still keep breathing. Fortunately, along with the dress, Winfrey wore an eye-catching $10,000 fox coat that had been dyed purple in honor of the movie's title.

When the Academy Awards were over, *The Color*

Oprah Winfrey was thrilled to make her film debut in the movie version of *The Color Purple,* one of her favorite books, written by Alice Walker. Winfrey's onscreen husband was played by actor Willard Pugh.

Purple came away without winning anything. To Winfrey and the rest of the cast, it was terribly disappointing. Yet she took her disappointment in stride. With her sense of humor intact, she said, "Perhaps God was saying to me, 'Oprah, you are not winning because your dress is too tight for you to make it up all those steps to receive the statuette.'"[7]

After *The Color Purple*, Winfrey realized how much she loved acting, and that she wanted to do more of it.[8] She also knew that she would be able to accept more acting roles if she had complete control of her talk show. That way she could adjust her schedule without having to get approval from the station.

Although she would not get ownership of her show for two more years, Winfrey did create her own company, called Harpo Productions, Inc., in 1986. (Harpo is Oprah spelled backward.) With that, she began to pave the way to achieving control of her show and her destiny. In the meantime, Harpo Productions handled Winfrey's ever-growing fan mail and much of the publicity for her show.

Now Winfrey was busy with her show, her acting career, and her new business. Yet she also wanted to do something to help people in her community. Always especially interested in helping children, she began a project called Little Sisters of Cabrini Green. Cabrini Green is a housing project in Chicago for low-income families. Winfrey knew of its reputation as a place where drug dealings, random killings, and violence were common. She thought many of the children living there could benefit from extra attention and guidance.

Winfrey and her staff at the show began visiting some of the girls at Cabrini Green. Over time they treated the girls to many different activities. Sometimes Winfrey would take them shopping or to the movies. Other times they went to the library. Once she even hosted a sleep over for her "little sisters."

Along with activities and attention, Winfrey also gave the girls the benefit of some of the lessons that had helped her. She told them about the importance of an education. Her only requirement for the girls to stay in the group was that they get good grades at school. It was just what her father had required of her years before.[9]

In 1986, Winfrey's life changed in yet another important way. She had not dated seriously since the devastating end of her last relationship in Baltimore. She was so busy with *A.M. Chicago* that it was hard to find the time. And whom would she date, anyway? With her growing wealth and fame, who would be able to maintain a balanced relationship with her? Later that year, Winfrey met the person who would take center stage in her life. That person was Stedman Graham.

Graham is a handsome, six-foot-six-inch former

basketball player. He grew up in New Jersey. Well educated, Graham has a master's degree in education from Ball State University in Muncie, Indiana. His quiet charm was a striking contrast to Winfrey's bubbling effervescence. He had previously been married for two years and had a daughter named Wendy who lived with her mother in Texas.

Winfrey and Graham had met from time to time at various civic and social events in Chicago. He was thirty-six; she was thirty-two. After two unsuccessful attempts, Graham finally persuaded Winfrey to meet him for a date. From the first, she was charmed. As she later said, "It had been a long time since I'd been treated kindly by a man."[10]

It was the beginning of a long-lasting relationship. Winfrey has called Graham her "rock" and speaks frequently of his kindness. Talking of Graham's loyalty and steadfastness in good times and bad, Winfrey says, "Lots of people want to ride with you in the limo. But you want someone who'll be there when the limo breaks down, who'll help you catch the bus."[11]

By this time, Winfrey's show had become so successful that the next logical step was to expand its viewing audience beyond the Chicago area. The time was right to broadcast Winfrey from coast to coast. To do that, she needed to strike a deal with a professional television syndicator. The syndicator's job would be to sell her show's broadcast rights to individual television stations across the nation. In return, Winfrey would receive part of the profits from the show's sales.

King World Productions, Inc., was the syndication company Winfrey chose to arrange nationwide broadcasting of her show. Owned and managed by Michael and Roger King, the company had built its reputation by syndicating game and talk shows. Two of its most well-known shows, *Jeopardy!* and *Wheel of Fortune*, had been extremely successful, making the Kings and their clients very wealthy.

First, the King brothers changed the show's name from *A.M. Chicago* to *The Oprah Winfrey Show*. WLS would continue to produce the show, and King World would sell it to as many stations as it could. With the help of her business manager, Jeffrey Jacobs, Winfrey negotiated a contract by which she would receive 24 percent of the show's earnings. With projected earnings of $125 million a year, Winfrey stood to become a multimillionaire very quickly.

To promote Winfrey, the King brothers showed tapes of some of her previous shows to stations all over the country. They let station managers know that from its start, Winfrey's show had consistently been beating *The Donahue Show* in the Chicago television ratings. On top of that, Winfrey's performance in *The Color Purple* gave her additional publicity. There were also many interviews with newspapers and magazines to promote the show.

This would be the first time an African-American woman had ever hosted a national television talk show. Some station managers were concerned for just that reason. Would racism become an issue? Would viewers decide not to watch *The Oprah Winfrey Show* just because Winfrey was African American?

When *The Oprah Winfrey Show* debuted on September 8, 1986, it was seen in 138 cities. The topic of the first show was "How to Choose a Mate." Her

As her Chicago talk show grew more and more popular, Winfrey created her own company, Harpo Productions, and decided to broadcast her show all over the nation.

guest was an author who had written a book about the subject. During that first week many people were eager to see how Winfrey would do against Donahue. As Donahue himself said in an interview, "I wish her luck, but not in my time slot!"[12]

Once again, Winfrey showed that she had what it took to dominate the talk show world. In almost every city where the two shows were shown on different stations at the same time, *The Oprah Winfrey Show* began to edge out Donahue. Viewers across the nation were warming to what one magazine described as "her enthusiasm, her honesty, and her sassy spirit."[13] *Ebony* magazine wrote about Winfrey's impact in this way: "Her effusive, off-the-cuff interview style has given a badly needed transfusion to the anemic talk-show format."[14]

How did Winfrey respond to her growing national success? She said, "Doing this show is my way of fulfilling myself. . . . It is a ministry, and it does what a ministry should do: uplift people, encourage them, and give them a sense of hope about themselves."[15]

With syndication, Winfrey's fame and income skyrocketed. By the end of the 1986 television season, Winfrey's share of the profits for *The Oprah Winfrey Show* had earned her $30 million. She now had plenty of money at her fingertips, but she budgeted herself only $1 million to spend in 1987. As she explained, "I can do that without worrying if this ends, will I have enough to eat."[16]

Winfrey began reaping the benefits of her hard work and success. In the summer of 1986, she bought a spectacular luxury condominium on the fifty-seventh floor of a high-rise apartment building in downtown Chicago. It cost $800,000 dollars. Providing a breath-taking view of the city and Lake Michigan, her new home featured marble floors and a crystal chandelier in her bedroom closet. In the bathroom, water flowed into a marble bathtub from a gold faucet shaped like a swan. Winfrey turned one room into a media center with a huge television screen and a built-in stereo sys-tem. The condo also had a library for her many books.

Generous by nature, Winfrey turned to her parents. She wanted to use her money to make their lives better. Winfrey's mother, Vernita Lee, was still living in Milwaukee. First, Winfrey bought her a condominium there. Then she set up a generous monthly allowance for her mother, so she would never have to work again.

Winfrey also wanted to repay her father for his efforts in guiding her life. But Vernon Winfrey was harder to help. The problem was, he really did not want anything. He was satisfied with his life as it was.[17] Stubbornly, Winfrey would not take no for an answer. Finally, Vernon said he supposed he could use some new tires for his truck. Later, he added that a bigger television for his barbershop would also be nice. That way, more of his customers could watch his daughter on her show as they got their hair cut. And finally, he really would be delighted if Winfrey could get him tickets to the Mike Tyson–Tyrell Biggs boxing match in October 1987.

Winfrey happily granted her father's wishes. Soon he had new tires for his truck and a television set so big that the screen could easily be seen from any spot in the barbershop. She also flew her father to Las Vegas, Nevada, for the big fight. To this day, Vernon Winfrey still lives in the little brick home of Winfrey's teenage years. The only apparent difference is the light blue Mercedes-Benz sedan—another gift from his daughter—parked in the driveway.

The past two years had been spectacular for Winfrey. "Right now, I feel about as good as you can feel and still live," she said.[18] Her success was virtually unparalleled. Yet after coming so far so quickly, how long could she expect such good fortune to last?

8

Taking Care of Business

y May 1987, *The Oprah Winfrey Show* had been on national television for nine months. Just as in Chicago, it had immediately become a popular hit with viewers across the country. Professionally, Winfrey was a huge success. Yet on the personal front, she had some unfinished business to address.

Winfrey knew that her lack of a college degree was still on her father's mind. She had moved to Baltimore in 1976 without completing her work at Tennessee State University. She had finished all her courses, but not her senior project, so she had never received her degree.

Vernon Winfrey felt that no matter how wealthy and famous his daughter had become, she still needed to finish her college education.[1] She had so little left to do compared with the four years of work she had already invested.

So Oprah Winfrey reenrolled at Tennessee State University and completed her final project. In May 1987, she traveled back to Nashville and received her bachelor's degree. She also gave the commencement speech at the graduation ceremony.

At the same time, Winfrey announced that she would be funding ten scholarships to the university. Each one would be worth $77,000. The scholarships would be awarded based on students' financial needs as well as their scholastic ability. According to the rules Winfrey set up, once a student received one of her scholarships, he or she would have to maintain at least a B average to keep it.

Winfrey wanted to personally handle the scholarship funds. She would choose the recipients, monitor their progress, and pay for everything they needed. But, she warned, "The minute their grades drop, they're out, because they have no excuse."[2] To honor her father, Winfrey gave the scholarships in Vernon Winfrey's name. She still contributes $250,000 each year to replenish the fund.

The next month would also bring Winfrey a special honor. *The Oprah Winfrey Show* was by then so successful that it was a major contender at the Daytime Emmy Awards. Winning an Emmy Award is a high honor for any television program. The awards are like the Academy Awards except that instead of focusing on movies, they highlight the best television programs shown during the day. The attention the winning shows receive may also increase the number of viewers.

When *The Oprah Winfrey Show* swept the talk show categories at the 1987 Daytime Emmy Awards, it was quite a victory for Winfrey and her crew. The show won awards for the best talk show, the best talk show host,

Vernon Winfrey's barbershop and general store in east Nashville. Oprah credits her father's strict but loving manner with turning her life around during her teen years.

and the best talk show director. The awards clearly affirmed her show's success and popularity.

Winfrey's life was hectic with activities, but her love of reading continued to be a constant source of pleasure and relaxation for her. Always on the lookout for stories of courage to recommend to her friends, she discovered *The Women of Brewster Place* by Gloria Naylor. She had begun reading it while filming *The Color Purple*. The story is about the joys and hardships of seven African-American women who live in a tenement building on Brewster Place in a northern city. As Winfrey described it, "The book makes a great statement for maintaining your dignity in a world that tries to strip you of it."[3]

By 1988, an idea had taken shape in Winfrey's mind to make a television movie based on the book. At first she had trouble finding a network that was willing to show it. Turned down by ABC, CBS, and NBC, Winfrey did not give up. She finally convinced an executive at ABC to read the book. Impressed with the story, he agreed with Winfrey that it was right for television. ABC then agreed to do a miniseries.

Filming began at Universal Studios in Hollywood in April 1988. The four-hour miniseries would star Cicely Tyson, Paul Winfield, Robin Givens, and . . . Oprah Winfrey. As Mattie Michael, one of the seven women of Brewster Place, Winfrey was cast in her first starring role.

Just as she had wished for the role of Sofia, Winfrey was eager to play Mattie. She said, "After *The Color Purple*, I wanted to prove my acting was not a fluke."[4] Winfrey prepared for the role by creating a two-hundred-page journal as if Mattie had written it herself. "I tried to build a life for her. I thought about who her friends would be, where she would have gone to school, what her interests might be."[5] It was a huge job, but the effort let her immerse herself in the part.

When *The Women of Brewster Place* was aired the next year, it drew a large audience. Winfrey's fans wanted to see their favorite talk show host in an acting role. Although the show received mixed reviews, ABC was pleased with its quality and ratings. They agreed to develop a weekly series based on the show.

In the meantime, Winfrey continued her talk show. At work, she was known for her dedication and for expecting excellence from those who work with her. To produce her show and manage all the details of her career and her life, Winfrey needed a group of people dedicated to her success. Over the years she has built just such a close-knit group of people around her. They not only work for her; some have become her dear friends.[6]

Many of Winfrey's closest staff are young, single women. Their attention to their boss often goes beyond professional courtesy. In many ways, Winfrey's staff is like a family, offering support and advice when

Oprah Winfrey as Mattie Michael in the TV series *Brewster Place.* Winfrey persuaded ABC to make a television movie and then to develop a television series based on Gloria Naylor's book *The Women of Brewster Place.*

she needs it. As her producer, Mary Kay Clinton, once said in describing her loyalty to Winfrey, "I would take a bullet for her."[7]

For her part, Winfrey treasures her staff and takes a personal interest in them. She rewards them well for their hard work and thoughtfulness. She has been known to give her closest staff outlandishly generous gifts. She has sent some on exotic vacations and has taken others on extravagant shopping sprees. Still others have been given large amounts of cash, diamond earrings, cars, and luggage with travel gift certificates enclosed. One year she gave Debra DiMaio, her executive producer and close friend, a year's certificate for one dinner each month with friends in different cities around the world—all expenses paid. As Winfrey said in an interview, "Yes, I'm very generous. . . . I'd love to get a present from me!"[8]

To many people, Winfrey's life must have seemed perfect. After all, by 1988 she was only thirty-four years old and had become a national celebrity. She had enough money to buy just about anything she wanted, and her success showed no signs of slowing down.

Yet like all people, Winfrey did have problems. One issue that had haunted her for years was her weight. Since her time in Baltimore, Winfrey's weight had slowly but steadily increased, and she was unhappy about it. "I've gained 70 pounds since I first started dieting," she was known to say.[9]

In 1988, Winfrey began a strict diet. Choosing a liquid diet plan, she ate no solid food for three and a half months. During that time she only drank liquid meals that she purchased. Because of the extreme limitations of this program, Winfrey remained under strict medical supervision throughout the diet. She also exercised regularly by jogging in the mornings and evenings. By October 17 she had lost sixty-seven pounds.

Many people still remember *The Oprah Winfrey Show* on November 15, 1988. That was the day Winfrey announced her dieting results to her television audience. Winfrey triumphantly revealed her new figure in a pair of slim-fitting, size 10 designer jeans. The last time she had worn them was in 1982. She also rolled out a child's red wagon filled with sixty-seven pounds of animal fat. Her audience could clearly see how much fat had disappeared from her body.

Although Winfrey did not know it then, her struggle to control her weight was far from over. Her happiness and pride of that day would slip away as the pounds began to creep back. But for the moment, Winfrey tasted the sweet satisfaction of success.

Winfrey also continued to expand her business interests into 1988. First, she took the steps necessary to gain ownership of *The Oprah Winfrey Show*. It had been her dream for the past two years. After Harpo Productions took over the show, the company rented it to WLS-TV so the station could continue airing it.

Next, Winfrey spent $10 million to buy a production studio in Chicago. She named it Harpo Studios. Her eye always on the future, she knew that having her own studio meant she could tape her show and televise it later. That way her schedule would be more flexible, and she could take on other projects when she wanted. She also hoped the studio would attract movie and television projects from Hollywood and New York, creating jobs for more people in Chicago.[10]

With Harpo Studios, Winfrey became the first African-American person, and only the third woman, ever to own a major film studio. The facility had previously been owned by Studio Networks and took up an entire city block near downtown Chicago. It included three large studios, an office, workshops for creating sets and props, screening rooms, a darkroom, a kitchen, and parking facilities.

After buying the studio, Winfrey quickly spent another $10 million to have it renovated into a first-rate facility. Harpo Studios opened on January 15, 1989. *The Oprah Winfrey Show* had a new home about one-half mile west of downtown Chicago.

Running her own studio was a new experience for Winfrey. With no formal training, she simply plunged in and began to learn on the job. Her business philosophy for Harpo Productions had been to "create an environment so stimulating that people will love coming to work."[11] She was determined to be a good boss and manager: "Fairness is my doctrine. If you operate on a doctrine of fairness you can survive and do very well."[12] Always interested in her employees and their happiness, she did not want anyone working for her who was not happy at the job.[13] At the same time, she also developed a reputation as a boss who demanded excellence from her employees. As one observer put it, "Oprah and her producers have always run their business like they're No. 5 rather than No. 1."[14]

Continuing to develop her business interests, Winfrey opened a restaurant with Richard Melman, a Chicago restaurateur, in early 1989. The Eccentric, created out of an old warehouse, served moderately priced meals. The unique eating establishment, which is no longer in business today, was like a combination of four restaurants. Each section featured the food and atmosphere of a different country. Customers could choose French, Italian, English, or American food. In the American section, the menu featured some of Winfrey's all-time favorites. One was Oprah's Potatoes, a mashed-potato dish flavored with horseradish, cream, and parsley.

Later that year Winfrey decided that she needed a home where she could get away from the hustle and pressure of her work in Chicago. She bought a 160-acre farm in Rolling Prairie, Indiana, about a two-hour drive from Chicago. The country setting provides an ideal escape. The house is built at the end of a long drive. A white fence separates it from the surrounding acres of pastureland for horses and sheep. The house, built of stone in an English Tudor style, has twelve bedrooms so Winfrey can have friends and family stay over whenever she wants. The mansion also includes a screening room and a library. On the grounds are tennis courts, a swimming pool, and horse stables. A tranquil pond provides a home for ducks and geese.

Winfrey's Indiana home became her favorite retreat. In describing it, she has said, "I've never loved a place the way I love my farm. I grew up in the country, which is probably why I'm so attached to the land. I love it. I love the lay of the land. I love walking the land. And I love knowing that it's my land."[15]

In 1989, Morehouse College in Atlanta, Georgia, awarded Winfrey with an honorary doctorate of humane letters. Winfrey donated $1 million to Morehouse to establish the Oprah Winfrey Endowment Scholarship Fund. It provides scholarships to students who have shown that they can do well in school but who need financial help for college.

Sadly, Winfrey saw 1989 end with the death of her half brother, Jeffrey, to AIDS. He was just twenty-nine years old and died a few days before Christmas. Yet as the new decade would prove, some of Winfrey's most difficult challenges lay just ahead.

9

FIGHTING DEMONS

By the start of 1990, *The Oprah Winfrey Show* was in its fourth season. It was still holding its place as the number-one television talk show in its time slot. It was making millions of dollars for its syndicators and for Winfrey herself. Roger and Michael King had also introduced *The Oprah Winfrey Show* internationally. It could be seen in such diverse countries as Japan, New Zealand, Canada, Thailand, and Saudi Arabia. The show was now syndicated to 20 million viewers around the world.

Yet problems soon clouded Winfrey's life. In March, a tabloid newspaper, the *National Enquirer*, revealed her long-held secret about her teenage pregnancy. When the story was also printed soon afterward in the widely read Sunday newspaper supplement *Parade*, this hidden piece of Winfrey's past became general knowledge.

Winfrey had always wanted to keep that part of her life secret. With it now exposed, she had to relive that terrible time. She also had to face her public. Winfrey agonized about her future. She was desperately afraid her fans would think she had betrayed them. She thought they would hate her when they found out about her baby.[1]

Winfrey's public, however, remained loyal to her. The storm passed and her popularity held. Winfrey was also able to find a positive side to the painful disclosure. Responding to the media attention about her abuse as a child, she was able to increase public awareness about that issue. Before long, she would also take action to help prevent child abuse for others.

In the meantime, *The Women of Brewster Place* television series debuted on ABC in May 1990. Unfortunately, the weekly show did not draw the large number of viewers the miniseries had attracted. The show was canceled after only four episodes.

Although Winfrey was disappointed, the show's cancellation was also a relief.[2] Adding another weekly show to her responsibilities for *The Oprah Winfrey Show* had made Winfrey's schedule unbearably hectic.

Without the series to occupy her time, she could focus exclusively on her talk show.

Early the next year, Winfrey was outraged to learn about the murder of a four-year-old Chicago girl named Angelica Mena. She had been molested and strangled, then thrown into Lake Michigan. Angelica's murderer was a convicted child abuser. The abuse Winfrey had endured as a child caused the tragedy of this little girl's suffering to strike a deep chord in her heart. As she recalled later, "I did not know the child, never heard her laughter. But I vowed that night to do something, to take a stand for the children of this country."[3]

By April, she had hired attorney James Thompson, a former Illinois governor, to draft a law that would create a national registry of convicted child abusers. The list would be available to schools and other employers who hired people to work with children. With the registry, they could make sure they did not unknowingly hire anyone who had been convicted of harming children.

Senator Joseph Biden, a Democrat from Delaware, agreed to sponsor the bill in Congress. Hearings to discuss the bill's merits were held on November 12, 1991, in Washington, D.C., before the Senate Judiciary Committee. People were asked to explain to the committee why such a registry was so badly needed.

Oprah Winfrey was one of the main witnesses that

day. Carefully choosing her words, she forcefully explained her experiences at the hands of child abusers. She wanted the members of the Senate Judiciary Committee to understand the helplessness of children in defending themselves. Speaking with conviction, she told the committee, "You lose your childhood when you've been abused. My heart goes out to those children who are abused at home and have no one to turn to."[4]

Although it would take two more years, Winfrey's efforts were finally rewarded. The National Child Protection Act—nicknamed the "Oprah bill" because of her leadership in getting it introduced before Congress—would become law in December 1993.

In the spring of 1991, Winfrey added another home to her holdings. This time, she bought eighty-five acres of land in picturesque Telluride, Colorado. Nestled in the Rocky Mountains, the little town of Telluride is a popular ski resort. Along with the land, Winfrey's purchase included a luxurious log-and-stone chalet with a spectacular mountain view from her dining room. During the ski season, skiers on a nearby ski lift often wave and shout greetings to her as they ride by.

Winfrey's weight also continued to be a concern for her throughout 1991. After her sixty-seven-pound loss in 1988, the weight had started reappearing with frightening speed. By February 1991, she had gained eighty-seven pounds.

Frustrated and discouraged, Winfrey decided to try again. This time she would do things differently. Instead of eliminating solid food and losing weight too quickly, Winfrey chose a slower, more stable approach. In May she visited a weight-reduction center in southern California, called Cal-a-Vie. There she met chef Rosie Daley. Winfrey thought the delicious low-fat meals Daley created were just what she needed at home. What if Daley could cook for her all the time?

It took a lot of convincing, but Winfrey finally persuaded Daley to move to Chicago. She became Winfrey's personal cook and nutritionist in September 1991. Over time, with Daley's help, Winfrey's weight began to stabilize.

The next year, while at her Indiana farm, Stedman Graham formally proposed marriage to Winfrey. Without hesitation, she accepted. Winfrey and Graham planned their wedding for September 8, 1993. She chose that date for sentimental reasons—it was her father's wedding date. Winfrey made an appointment with Oscar de la Renta, the famous clothing designer, so they could begin planning her wedding gown. Soon, however, the couple decided to put aside their wedding plans. Today, they are still together, but no wedding date has been set.

In 1993, with her fortieth birthday looming just a year away, Winfrey decided she would like to write the story of her life. With the help of a professional writer,

Oprah Winfrey and her fiancé, Stedman Graham.

Joan Barthel, Winfrey began the task. She wanted her book to be more than simply a record of the events in her life. She wanted the book's message to match the message of her show—to inspire people to take control of their lives rather than allowing events to control them.[5]

The deal would be a fantastic one for her lucky publisher, Alfred A. Knopf. A book by Oprah Winfrey was practically guaranteed to be a best-seller, making millions of dollars. With a lot of publicity, Winfrey appeared in June in Miami Beach, Florida, at the American Booksellers Convention to promote her book.

Just two weeks later, Winfrey announced her difficult decision to put the project on hold. As she explained, "[The book] was really wonderfully written . . . great detail and all that, but *what did it all mean?*"[6] If her book did not convey the message she intended, Winfrey preferred to keep it a private project.

During the time she was working with Barthel, Winfrey's weight reached an all-time high. Despite her healthier eating habits with chef Rosie Daley, she needed something else to help her control her weight. She turned to Bob Greene, an exercise physiologist and personal trainer, for help. She had met him the previous summer in Colorado at the Doral Telluride Resort and Spa. As she had with Rosie Daley, Winfrey used her powers of persuasion with Greene. He soon moved to Chicago so he could work with her every day.

Training with Greene, Winfrey's perspective about her weight began to change. She began to uncover many of the underlying reasons she chose to overeat in the first place. With Green's help she also changed her vision. Instead of focusing just on weight, her goal was to become fit, healthy, and strong. She realized that if she concentrated on exercise and fitness, the weight loss would happen automatically.

Under Greene's direction, Winfrey added an aggressive physical conditioning plan to her healthy eating habits. At its most rigorous, her daily workout consisted of an eight-mile run, a forty-five-minute workout on a stair-climbing machine, and up to 350 sit-ups. Bob Greene observed Winfrey's progress this way: "Obviously appearance is part of it, but she's realized the power she gains from getting up and training every morning. That power extends to other parts of her life as well, not just the physical."[7] Over time, Winfrey's hard work paid off. By mid-November 1993, she had lost eighty-seven pounds.

That month, Winfrey's next television movie was aired on ABC-TV. *There Are No Children Here* is based on the national best-selling book by Alex Kotlowitz. It is the true story of an African-American family fighting to survive in the violent, drug-infested Henry Horner housing project in Chicago. Winfrey played the main character, LaJoe Rivers. Her close friend and mentor, Maya Angelou, played LaJoe's mother. In the story, LaJoe knows that she is raising her sons in a dangerous environment. She dreams of moving her family to a safer place.

Winfrey had often driven past the Henry Horner housing project on her way to work. The movie was filmed right there, and during that time Winfrey got to know many of the residents. Speaking later of the experience, she said, "I used to see these kids from the projects walking down the street and think, 'Oh, my God, is something going to happen?' Now I look to see if it's one of the kids I know. That's the difference."[8]

Winfrey earned $500,000 for starring in the movie. She donated all her earnings to establish a scholarship fund for the students living at Henry Horner. The ABC television network later donated an equal amount to the scholarship fund.

Also in November, Winfrey featured her cook, Rosie Daley, on *The Oprah Winfrey Show*. During the program, she and Daley demonstrated how to prepare some of Winfrey's favorite low-fat dishes. As a result of that show, Daley wrote a cookbook, which was published the next year. *In the Kitchen with Rosie: Oprah's Favorite Recipes* was an immediate best-seller. It became the fastest-selling hardcover book in history.[9] Winfrey viewed the book's success this way: "I had been dieting ten years straight on TV. People saw this book as the answer."[10] She contributed to the project by appearing on the book's cover and by writing an introduction. The pages of the book are also peppered with her comments.

In 1994, *The Oprah Winfrey Show* continued at the top of the daytime talk show popularity charts, although ratings were beginning to slip. Also, unknown to most of her audience, there were signs of unrest within Harpo Productions. Oprah's staff was devoted to her, but the stress of the company's fast-paced schedule and many business interests began to

One reason for her success, says Oprah Winfrey, is that "people sense the realness."

take a toll on the employees. As one producer described it: "They [her staff] give their lives to her. People who work there get divorced, put off having kids, have no outside lives. Because everything, all your time and energy, is given to Oprah."[11] There were conflicts among employees, and several producers and staff members left the show, including the executive producer, Debra DiMaio.

Winfrey's fairness doctrine was no longer enough to run her company effectively. Recalling that time, she later said, "Being a boss is tough. I used to believe I could handle things just by being fair or doing the best I knew how. But I learned that, in fact, that is not necessarily enough."[12]

At the same time, there were other issues affecting *The Oprah Winfrey Show*. Since the syndication of Winfrey's show in 1986, the number of talk shows on television had increased. In the never-ending competition for viewers, the shows' topics had become increasingly outlandish. To many, they were downright offensive. Ranging from the ridiculous to the bizarre, talk shows were parading before their audiences a steady stream of child molesters, adulterers, and social misfits. The topics often revolved around such issues as deviant sexual behavior, spousal abuse, child pornography, and criminal behavior. Some talk shows aired what became known as "confrontational TV," in which victims of one sort or another confronted their abusers, often provoking ridicule and harassment from the audience.

Because of their trend to offensive and controversial topics, talk shows got a bad reputation. They were commonly referred to as "trash television" by critics, and many people thought the situation was out of control. They considered talk show content not only inappropriate and degrading, but actually harmful to both guests and viewers.

In a study published in *The Journal of Popular Culture* in 1994, professors Vicki Abt and Mel Seesholtz of Pennsylvania State University compared the 1960s *Donahue Show*, which emphasized celebrity interviews, with the 1990s version, saying, "Today's *Donahue Show* is a relentless display of deviants, conflict and personal stories of real-life private people trying to 'fix themselves' through therapy."[13] They put *The Oprah Winfrey Show* in the same category.

According to Abt and Seesholtz, on talk shows the distinctions between right and wrong may begin to fade: "We the viewing audience have entertained ourselves at the disasters of real lives. . . . This is one of the more shameless aspects of the talk show spectacle. . . . We consume others' misfortunes without feeling any responsibility to do anything to intervene."[14]

Reporters often asked Winfrey to respond to those who criticized her show. She cited the many letters she was getting from people who had watched her show and decided to make an important change in their lives.[15] She has also said that she wanted people with problems to know that they are not alone.[16] Some people also defended talk shows by saying that they were simply a window into the good and bad of American culture.

Winfrey is sometimes accused of creating the trend toward trash TV. She has had her share of controversial shows, including "Adoption Rejection" (April 19, 1988), "Priestly Sins" (October 7, 1992), and "Who Does Baby Michael Belong To?" (October 26, 1993). Despite the criticism, Winfrey has always maintained that her show and the way it dealt with "trash" topics was different from the others. She said, "My philosophy has been that people deserve to come and to leave [my show] with their dignity. I never did what you see on the air today—nowhere close to it—because I never wanted people to be humiliated and embarrassed."[17] Winfrey consistently held that the purpose of her show was to send a spiritual message to its viewers, that "you are responsible for your life."[18]

Nevertheless, after the 1994 season, Winfrey took a hard look at her show and decided to take a stand against sensational television. She said, "I am embarrassed by how far over the line [talk show] topics have gone, but I also recognize my own contribution to this." Recalling one especially bad show, she added, "People should not be surprised and humiliated on national television for the purpose of entertainment. I was ashamed of myself."[19]

Winfrey wanted to redirect her show's focus to topics that could help improve people's lives. She said, "The time has come for this genre of talk shows to move on from dysfunctional whining and complaining and blaming. I have had enough of people's dysfunction."[20] Instead, she wanted her viewers to feel affirmed, encouraged, better informed, and uplifted as a result of seeing her show. As she put it, "We need shows with images of life as we would like it to be. We need to ask programmers for positive role models for ourselves and our children, for television that will strengthen the human spirit."[21]

As for the show's ratings, they had indeed dropped since the 1992–1993 season. Even so, in 1995 *The Oprah Winfrey Show* still held its position as the number-one daytime talk show. As one television executive noted, "People just like spending an hour with her."[22]

In October 1995, Winfrey joined the information superhighway by establishing a Website for her show, <www.oprah.com>, on the Internet. Today she also has a Website on America Online, called "Oprah Online," which has become extremely popular with her fans.

The year 1996 brought yet another blockbuster book publication from Winfrey. Since late 1993 she had continued to manage her weight and to maintain her exercise routine with her trainer, Bob Greene. This time, she and Greene wrote a book together called *Make the Connection—Ten Steps to a Better Body and a Better Life*. As with Rosie Daley's book, *Make the Connection* shot straight to the top of *The New York Times* best-seller list.

The book contains Winfrey's personal records and reflections about her long struggle with her weight. As she explains, "Making the connection means understanding it's not about food . . . it's about how you live your life. . . ."[23] A companion book, *A Journal of Daily Renewal*, was published at the same time. Filled with inspirational quotations and advice, the book provides space to record progress while working on developing a healthy lifestyle.

In the book Winfrey describes how the peak of her training and effort came with her participation in the Marine Corps Marathon in Washington, D.C., in October 1994. Beforehand, she had set a personal goal to complete a marathon by her forty-first birthday. With her birthday just three months away, she would be ready. Running in the rain on the day of the marathon—in everything from a soft drizzle to a steady downpour—Winfrey met her goal. As she sloshed through puddles along the route, she could see homemade posters here and there from the sidelines saying, "Go Oprah!" or "We ♥ Oprah." She

Winfrey, whose weight has bounced up and down over the years, learned to expand her focus from food to fitness. Here, she is about to run the twenty-six-mile Marine Corps Marathon.

finished the race in just under four and a half hours, calling it "truly one of the best moments of my life."[24]

In 1996, Winfrey found another way to make her show stand out. With her lifelong interest in reading, it was natural for her to begin a book club for her viewers, though the idea did not begin with her. When her producers had first suggested it, Winfrey thought it would not work. She said, "I thought we would die in the ratings. I thought they had lost their minds."[25]

But after mulling over the suggestion, she decided to give it a try. Announced at the beginning of the

The publishing industry was delighted when Winfrey started a book club for her television viewers. These are just a few of the titles she has featured on her show. The books Winfrey selects for her book club become instant best-sellers.

1996–1997 television season, the book club served Winfrey's purpose: to get more people to read. As she said, "My idea is to re-introduce reading to people who've forgotten it exists."[26]

An avid reader since girlhood, Winfrey sees the value of books in this way: "I feel strongly that, no matter who you are, reading opens doors and provides, in your own personal sanctuary, an opportunity to explore and feel things, the way other forms of media cannot. I want books to become part of my audience's lifestyle, for reading to become a natural phenomenon with them, so that it is no longer a big deal."[27]

Each month during the show's season she recommended one of her favorite books to her viewers. For her first selection, she chose *The Deep End of the Ocean* by Jacqueline Mitchard. It is about the kidnapping of a three-year-old boy.

With Oprah's Book Club, Winfrey's goal of encouraging more people to read was fulfilled. Roger Riger of *Publishing Trends* estimated that during the book club's first year, Winfrey's recommendations were responsible for the sale of 12 million books. Many local reading clubs have also sprung up around the country as a result of her example.

What she may not have expected was that every one of her book recommendations would instantly become a best-seller. The pattern began with *The Deep End of the Ocean*. Describing the phenomenon, *Newsweek* magazine reported: "When Oprah held up a copy of the book and told her television audience, 'You all are going to have to buy it,' that is just what they did."[28] Winfrey's ability to inspire the trust and loyalty of her viewers had become a powerful force. In fact, Winfrey's influence has become so broad that a term has been created for it. Called the "Oprah Effect," it refers to the power of her influence on society.

In 1996, the beef industry claimed that the "Oprah Effect" was responsible for a drop in cattle prices. On April 16, 1996, the topic on *The Oprah Winfrey Show* was dangerous foods. Winfrey's purpose was to educate her audience about possible food-related health risks. A guest, Howard Lyman, was there to inform the public about the possibility of getting mad cow disease, a disease that infects and destroys the brain. Although no cases of mad cow disease had ever been reported in the United States, his warning got Winfrey's attention. She said, "It has just stopped me cold from eating another burger." Beef prices began dropping the day of the show and continued to go down for two weeks. Some called it the "Oprah Crash" of 1996.[29]

For people who raise beef cattle for a living, the drop in prices was a disaster. Some people in the beef industry lost millions of dollars. A group of four beef producers blamed Winfrey and decided to sue her for $10 million. The trial was held in Amarillo, Texas, two years later. Winfrey's lawyers successfully argued that the drop in beef prices was due to drought and high feed prices rather than the content of Winfrey's show. The beef producers lost their case.

As 1996 came to a close, Oprah Winfrey could look back on her life's accomplishments with tremendous satisfaction. After ten years, *The Oprah Winfrey Show* was still the nation's number-one daytime television talk show. She had earned the respect of her colleagues and the devotion of her huge audience. Along with that, Winfrey was named the highest-paid entertainer by *Forbes* magazine. It appeared that she had won her battle with her weight. She had also dealt with the demons of her abuse as a child. What was left for Oprah Winfrey to tackle?

10

MAKING A
DIFFERENCE

n 1997, *The Oprah Winfrey Show*, broadcast in 205 television markets across the country, was the highest-rated talk show in television history. At the 1997 Daytime Emmys, *The Oprah Winfrey Show* received its fourth consecutive Daytime Emmy Award for Outstanding Talk Show. With the five other Emmys it received that evening, the show could now boast having won thirty Daytime Emmy Awards since its national debut in 1986.

Yet with all its triumphs, the question of the show's future began to loom. As the twelfth season began, Winfrey's fans anxiously awaited her decision: Would she continue *The Oprah Winfrey Show*? They knew she had given the question a lot of thought. After all, she had been doing 220 shows each year for more than ten years. It was rumored that her current season might be her last.

On October 16, Winfrey delighted her fans by announcing that she would continue the show for at least two more seasons. That would take *The Oprah Winfrey Show* into the year 2000. Explaining her decision, she said, "I've thought long and hard about the reality of doing four hundred more shows. I want to use television not only to entertain, but to help people lead better lives. I realize now, more than ever, that the show is the best way to accomplish these goals."[1]

Winfrey was also working on a number of film projects, devoting more time to her favorite career interest—acting. Harpo Productions was producing six made-for-television movies in a series called "Oprah Winfrey Presents," which would be aired over a three-year period. With her movies, as with her book club, Winfrey wants to expose the public to fine literature. She also hopes to make people more aware of the African-American experience and heritage. As she explained, "We look for projects that show individuals being responsible for themselves. It's all about seeing human beings as active creators of their lives rather than as passive victims."[2]

Winfrey's first television movie presentation, *Before*

Winfrey produced and starred in the 1997 television movie *Before Women Had Wings*, based on the book by Connie May Fowler.

Women Had Wings, premiered in November 1997. It was based on the 1996 book by Connie May Fowler and starred Winfrey and Ellen Barkin. The story is about a little girl named Bird Jackson who grows up in an abusive, poverty-stricken environment. Winfrey's next production aired in February 1998. *The Wedding* is based on a novel by Dorothy West and stars Halle Berry. Set in 1993 in Massachusetts, *The Wedding* explores the racial and social barriers that mar a young couple's wedding preparations. Other movies in the Oprah Winfrey Presents series include a remake of *David and Lisa*, about two emotionally disturbed teenagers who fall in love, and an adaptation of the book *Tuesdays With Morrie*, the true story of a man's weekly visits with his former college professor, who is dying of a fatal disease.

Winfrey's mission has expanded far beyond television and movies. Ever interested in using her influence to help others, she had introduced "Oprah's Angel Network" on September 17, 1997, telling her television audience, "I want you to open your hearts and see the world in a different way. I promise this will change your life for the better."[3]

The focus of Oprah's Angel Network was on making small changes that create big differences in people's lives. She had several ways to reach this goal. The first involved Habitat for Humanity. Made famous by President Jimmy Carter's participation, Habitat for Humanity uses donations and volunteers to build houses nationwide for people with low incomes. Winfrey's goal is to build one "Oprah house" in more than two hundred cities throughout the United States. She has encouraged businesses and viewers to participate in the project by donating materials and time. To kick off the project, Winfrey presented Habitat for Humanity with a check for $55,000 to pay for the first house.

Winfrey also started the "World's Largest Piggy Bank." She told her viewers, "Start collecting all the pennies, nickels, dimes, and quarters lying around the house, underneath the cushions, in the pillowcases. No bills . . . no checks. Just coins."[4] The money she collected was used to fund scholarships for needy, able students. Winfrey believes that "education is freedom, and that is one way you can make a huge difference in someone's life."[5]

Winfrey encouraged her network of angels to create little miracles by helping others in any way they could—and her viewers responded. They have sent her hundreds of stories telling her ways they have reached out to help the less fortunate in their communities. Winfrey has also encouraged her viewers to make a positive difference by volunteering in schools.

In addition to Oprah's Angel Network, Winfrey threw her support behind another charitable organization that she believes will have a long-lasting, positive impact. Called "A Better Chance," the charity finds talented minority students and funds their education at one of the country's top college preparatory high schools. Over the past thirty-five years, A Better Chance has helped more than ten thousand students get into college by providing them with the high school academic background and opportunity they need to succeed.

When Winfrey produced her first home video in 1997, she announced that all profits from the video would be donated to A Better Chance. In the video, called *Oprah Winfrey—Make the Connection*, Winfrey let the world into her private life as never before. The video shows her daily routine, her workout, her meals, and her preparation for the show. Its focus is on her long struggle with her weight.

Winfrey also wants people to think more about their blessings. Calling it her "Oprah Online Gratitude Family," Winfrey said, "If you focus on what you have, you'll end up having more. If you focus on what you lack, you will never have enough."[6] She encourages people to keep a "gratitude journal," just as she does. "At the end of the day, I write down five things that I'm grateful for, whether it's tasting the best mango sorbet or watching my dogs [cocker spaniels Sophie and Solomon] play in the park," she said.[7] Her goal is to have one million people throughout the country keeping gratitude journals.

Today Winfrey believes that the era of trash

television is coming to an end, but she says it served a purpose in overcoming the "disillusion that everybody else's life is happier than ours."[8] She now uses some of her shows to present what she calls "Change Your Life TV." Not all viewers are happy with this, and she loses many viewers each time she broadcasts one of these shows. On her America Online message board, "Oprah Online," a former fan called her "a preacher bent on having people think the way you do."[9]

Winfrey's life remains as busy as ever. Her typical day starts at five-thirty in the morning with a workout. By nine o'clock she greets her first studio audience of the day for the first of two tapings of *The Oprah Winfrey*

Thousands of people visit Harpo Studios in Chicago each year, eager to be a part of Winfrey's studio audience.

Show. The afternoon is often filled with meetings to discuss new show ideas or other business. After that, she tackles her second daily workout. After returning phone calls, Winfrey usually turns out her office lights between eight and nine in the evening. She spends as many weekends as she can at her Indiana farm, but usually takes work with her.

In October 1998, Winfrey's feature film *Beloved*, based on the Pulitzer Prize–winning novel by Toni Morrison, opened with great fanfare. Winfrey had her heart set on this project from the minute she read Morrison's book in 1987. The film was coproduced by Harpo and the Walt Disney Company and was directed by Academy Award–winner Jonathan Demme. Winfrey stars in the movie and was also involved in every aspect of the production. *Beloved*, the story of a runaway slave who is haunted by the spirit of her dead child, powerfully illustrates the horrors of slavery. "What I wanted to do is what Toni Morrison said: let people know what slavery felt like and not just what it looked like. Did I want it to be brutal? Yes. Did I want people to come out feeling a sense of devastation? Yes," said Winfrey.[10]

In its October 1998 issue, *Fortune* magazine named Oprah Winfrey the second most powerful woman in American business, saying, "Her power is her influence—over the entertainment industry, the book-publishing business, mass culture."[11] Despite her power and her success—Winfrey is said to be worth $550 million—she maintains an intensely spiritual life, with daily prayer and Bible reading. According to Winfrey, "I believe there is a spirit—call it holy, call it good, call it God—that works for my highest good always."[12]

Winfrey's impact on her audience has been immense. Through her courage, optimism, and honesty, Winfrey has tried to make better lives possible for her viewers. Since her earliest days, she has held the same theme for her work: "My mission is to use this position, power and money to create opportunities for other people."[13] She sees her work as a way of helping others while fulfilling her life's potential. Her success was honored by her peers when she received a Lifetime Achievement Award at the 1998 Daytime Emmy Awards. Her former competitor, Phil Donahue, presented the award to Winfrey, saying, "Your good works have touched all of us."[14]

Oprah Winfrey's journey has taken her a long way from her roots with Hattie Mae Lee on a tiny farm in Kosciusko, Mississippi. When Winfrey was asked, "What is your dream in life?" She said: "My dream is to fulfill my potential, whatever that may be or whatever form it takes as a human being on the planet. That's it, every day. I want to fulfill my potential, and our potential is limitless."[15] For Oprah Winfrey, the possibilities in her future seem limitless indeed.

CHRONOLOGY

1954—Oprah Gail Winfrey is born in Kosciusko, Mississippi, on January 29.

1960—Moves to Milwaukee, Wisconsin, to live with her mother.

1968—Moves to Nashville, Tennessee, to live with her father.

1971—Hired by radio station WVOL in Nashville as a part-time announcer; graduates from East High School and enters Tennessee State University.

1972—Wins titles as Miss Black Nashville and Miss Black Tennessee.

1973—Becomes news coanchor at WTVF-TV, making her the first African American and the youngest woman news coanchor in Nashville.

1976—Becomes coanchor of the local evening news for WJZ-TV in Baltimore.

1978—Cohosts *People Are Talking* with Richard Sher in Baltimore, Maryland.

1984—Moves to Chicago, Illinois, to host *A.M. Chicago*.

1985—Wins the part of Sofia in *The Color Purple*.

1986—Nominated for an Academy Award for her supporting role in *The Color Purple*; Winfrey creates Harpo Productions, Inc.; *The Oprah Winfrey Show* is syndicated nationally.

1987—Receives a bachelor of science degree in speech from Tennessee State University; *The Oprah Winfrey Show* sweeps the Daytime Emmy Awards, winning the categories of best talk show, best talk show host, and best talk show director.

successful

1988—Serves as coexecutive producer and stars in a lead role in the miniseries *The Women of Brewster Place*; Harpo Productions, Inc., buys *The Oprah Winfrey Show*; Winfrey buys a production studio in Chicago, Illinois, which becomes Harpo Studios.

1989—Co-owner of The Eccentric restaurant, which opens in Chicago; awarded an honorary doctorate of humane letters by Morehouse College; half brother, Jeffrey, dies.

1991—Testifies before the Senate Judiciary Committee in support of the National Child Protection Act; hires Rosie Daley as a personal cook and nutritionist.

1993—Hires Bob Greene as a personal trainer; produces and stars in television movie *There Are No Children Here*; the National Child Protection Act becomes law.

1994—*In the Kitchen with Rosie* is published.

1996—*Make the Connection—Ten Steps to a Better Body and a Better Life* is published; announces the beginning of "Oprah's Book Club."

1997—Produces and stars in television movie *Before Women Had Wings*; starts Oprah's Angel Network; produces home video *Oprah Winfrey—Make the Connection*.

1998—Produces and stars in the feature film *Beloved*; receives a Lifetime Achievement Award at the Daytime Emmys.

CHAPTER NOTES

Chapter 1. Day of Disaster

1. *Oprah—Make the Connection*, Harpo Video, Inc., Buena Vista Home Video, 1997.

2. Jill Brooke Coiner, "Oprah Sets the Record Straight," *McCall's*, November 1993, p. 200.

3. Chris Andersen, "Meet Oprah Winfrey," *Good Housekeeping*, August 1986, p. 37.

4. Leslie Rubenstein, "Oprah! Thriving on Faith," *McCall's*, August 1987, p. 140.

5. Richard Zoglin, "People Sense the Realness," *Time*, September 15, 1986, p. 99.

6. "Oprah Interview," *Real Life with Jane Pauley*, NBC-TV, September 6, 1991.

7. Zoglin, p. 99.

Chapter 2. A Gifted Child

1. *Oprah—Make the Connection*, Harpo Video, Inc., Buena Vista Home Video, 1997.

2. Liz Smith, "Oprah Exhales," *Good Housekeeping*, October 1995, p. 187.

3. Alan Richman, "Oprah," *People*, January 12, 1987, p. 50.

4. Ibid.

5. Ibid., p. 58.

6. Marilyn Johnson, "Oprah Winfrey, A Life in Books," *Life*, September 1997, p. 48.

7. John Culhane, "Oprah Winfrey: How Truth Changed Her Life," *Reader's Digest*, February 1989, p. 102.

8. Susan L. Taylor, "An Intimate Talk with Oprah," *Essence*, August 1987, p. 113.

9. Audrey Edwards, "Oprah Winfrey, Stealing the Show," *Essence*, October 1986, p. 52.

10. Ibid.

11. Johnson, p. 48.

12. Richman, p. 50.

13. Taylor, p. 57.

Chapter 3. Dangerous Times

1. John Culhane, "Oprah Winfrey: How Truth Changed Her Life," *Reader's Digest*, February 1989, p. 102.

2. Joanna Powell, "I Was Trying to Fill Something Deeper," *Good Housekeeping*, October 1996, p. 82.

3. Alan Richman, "Oprah," *People*, January 12, 1987, p. 55.

4. Joan Barthel, "Oprah!" *Ms.*, August 1986, p. 56.

5. Marcia Ann Gillespie, "Oprah Takes All," *Ms.*, November 1988, p. 54.

6. Susan L. Taylor, "An Intimate Talk with Oprah," *Essence*, August 1987, p. 58.

7. Ibid.

Chapter 4. "The Grand Ole Oprah"

1. Interview with Diane Sawyer, *20/20*, ABC-TV News, October 25, 1998.

2. Laura B. Randolph, "Oprah Opens Up About Her Weight, Her Wedding and Why She Withheld the Book," *Ebony*, October 1993, p. 132.

3. John Culhane, "Oprah Winfrey: How Truth Changed Her Life," *Reader's Digest*, February 1989, p. 103.

4. Susan L. Taylor, "An Intimate Talk with Oprah," *Essence*, August 1987, p. 58.

5. Marilyn Johnson, "Oprah Winfrey, A Life in Books," *Life*, September 1997, p. 53.

6. Culhane, p. 103.

7. Author interview with Katherine Sneed, October 5, 1998.

8. Norman King, *Everybody Loves Oprah* (New York: William Morrow, 1987), p. 64.

9. Alan Richman, "Oprah," *People*, January 12, 1987, p. 56.

10. Ibid.

11. Mary-Ann Bendel, "TV's Super Women," *Ladies' Home Journal*, March 1988, p. 169.

12. Audrey Edwards, "Oprah Winfrey, Stealing the Show," *Essence*, October 1986, p. 52.

13. Ibid., pp. 52, 123.

Chapter 5. A Change in Plans

1. Richard Zoglin, "Lady with a Calling," *Time*, August 8, 1988, p. 64.

2. Chris Andersen, "Meet Oprah Winfrey," *Good Housekeeping*, August 1986, p. 37.

3. "Oprah Interview," *Real Life with Jane Pauley*, NBC-TV, September 6, 1991.

4. Andersen, p. 37.

5. Pamela Noel, "Lights! Camera! Oprah!" *Ebony*, April 1985, p. 100.

6. Jill Booke Coiner, "Oprah Sets the Record Straight," *McCall's*, November 1993, p. 201.

7. Oprah Winfrey, "Wind Beneath My Wings," *Essence*, June 1989, p. 46.

8. Joan Barthel, "Here Comes Oprah!" *Ms.*, August 1986, p. 48.

Chapter 6. Blast Off in Chicago

1. Alan Richman, "Oprah," *People*, January 12, 1987, p. 50.

2. Bob Greene and Oprah Winfrey, *Make the Connection* (New York: Hyperion, 1996), p. 6.

3. Leslie Rubinstein, "Oprah! Thriving on Faith," *McCall's*, August 1987, p. 140.

4. Pamela Noel, "Lights! Camera! Oprah!" *Ebony*, April 1985, p. 102.

5. Seth Stevenson, "Oprah Winfrey: A Love Letter to the Beef Hater," *Slate*, February 7, 1998, on the Internet at <http://www.slate.com/code/Compost/Compost.asp> (September 17, 1998).

6. Mary-Ann Bendel, "TV's Super Women," *Ladies' Home Journal*, March 1988, p. 125.

7. Richard Zoglin, "People Sense the Realness," *Time*, September 15, 1986, p. 99.

8. Audrey Edwards, "Oprah Winfrey, Stealing the Show!" *Essence*, October 1986, p. 123.

9. Paul Noglows, "Oprah, the Year of Living Dangerously," *Working Woman*, May 1994, p. 54.

10. Harry F. Waters with Patricia King, "Chicago's Grand New Oprah," *Newsweek*, December 31, 1984, p. 51.

Chapter 7. The Color of Success

1. Leslie Rubinstein, "Oprah! Thriving on Faith," *McCall's*, August 1987, p. 140.

2. Marilyn Johnson, "Oprah Winfrey, A Life in Books," *Life*, September 1997, p. 54.

3. Chris Andersen, "Meet Oprah Winfrey," *Good Housekeeping*, August 1986, p. 37.

4. Ibid.

5. Joan Barthel, "Here Comes Oprah!" *Ms.*, August 1986, p. 49.

6. David Ansen, "We Shall Overcome," *Newsweek*, December 30, 1985, p. 60.

7. Rubinstein, p. 140.

8. Charles Whitaker, "Oprah Winfrey, The Most Talked-About TV Talk Show Host," *Ebony*, March 1987, p. 44.

9. Barthel, p. 56.

10. Susan L. Taylor, "An Intimate Talk with Oprah," *Essence*, August 1987, p. 116.

11. "Oprah Winfrey," *People*, August 25, 1986, p. 69.

12. Andersen, p. 32.

13. Eric Sherman, "Oprah Winfrey's Success Story," *Ladies' Home Journal*, March 1987, p. 64.

14. Whitaker, p. 39.

15. Mary-Ann Bendel, "TV's Super Women," *Ladies' Home Journal*, March 1988, pp. 168–169.

16. Alan Richman, "Oprah," *People*, January 12, 1987, p. 50.

17. Barthel, p. 88.

18. Sherman, p. 68.

Chapter 8. Taking Care of Business

1. John Culhane, "Oprah Winfrey: How Truth Changed Her Life," *Reader's Digest*, February 1989, p. 105.

2. Mary-Ann Bendel, "TV's Super Women," *Ladies' Home Journal*, March 1988, p. 170.

3. Joanne Kaufman, "Oprah Goes Hollywood," *People*, June 13, 1988, p. 40.

4. Ibid., p. 42.

5. Linden Gross, "Oprah Winfrey, Wonder Woman," *Ladies' Home Journal*, December 1988, p. 42.

6. Joan Barthel, "Here Comes Oprah!" *Ms.*, August 1986, p. 88.

7. Jackie Rogers, "Understanding Oprah," *Redbook*, September 1993, p. 134.

8. "Oprah Interview," *Real Life with Jane Pauley*, NBC-TV, September 6, 1991.

9. Eric Sherman, "Oprah Winfrey's Success Story," *Ladies' Home Journal*, March 1987, p. 64.

10. Marcia Ann Gillespie, "Winfrey Takes All," *Ms.*, November 1988, p. 52.

11. Ibid., p. 54.

12. Ibid.

13. Fred Goodman, "Madonna and Oprah, the Companies They Keep," *Working Woman*, December 1991, p. 55.

14. Paul Noglows, "Oprah, the Year of Living Dangerously," *Working Woman*, May 1994, p. 55.

15. Pearl Cleage, "Walking in the Light," *Essence*, June 1991, p. 48.

Chapter 9. Fighting Demons

1. Laura B. Randolph, "Oprah Opens Up About Her Weight, Her Wedding and Why She Withheld the Book," *Ebony*, October 1993, p. 134.

2. Pearl Cleage, "Walking in the Light," *Essence*, June 1991, p. 48.

3. Mary H. J. Farrell, "Oprah's Crusade," *People*, December 2, 1991, p. 69.

4. Ibid.

5. Randolph, p. 132.

6. Melina Gerosa, "What Makes Oprah Run?" *Ladies' Home Journal*, November 1994, p. 280.

7. Emma Bland, "How Oprah's Changed Our World," *McCall's*, November 1998, p. 68.

8. Shelley Levitt, Luchina Fisher, and Barbara Kleban Mills, "Oprah's Mission," *People*, November 29, 1993, p. 106.

9. Marilyn Johnson, "Oprah Winfrey, A Life in Books," *Life*, September 1997, p. 60.

10. Jonathan Van Meter, "Oprah's Moment," *Vogue*, October 1998, p. 392.

11. Gretchen Reynolds, "The Oprah Myth," *TV Guide*, July 23, 1994, p. 11.

12. Gretchen Reynolds, "A Year to Remember—Oprah Grows Up," *TV Guide*, January 7, 1995, p. 16.

13. Vicki Abt and Mel Seesholtz, "The Shameless World of Phil, Sally and Oprah: Television Talk Shows and the Deconstructing of Society," *Journal of Popular Culture*, summer 1994, p. 200.

14. Ibid., p. 204.

15. David Rensin, "The Prime Time of Oprah Winfrey," *TV Guide*, May 16, 1992, p. 15.

16. Joan Barthel, "Here Comes Oprah!" *Ms.*, August 1986, p. 88.

17. Laura B. Randolph, "Oprah!" *Ebony*, July 1995, p. 23.

18. Susan L. Taylor, "An Intimate Talk with Oprah," *Essence*, August 1987, p. 58.

19. Oprah Winfrey, "What We All Can Do to Change TV," *TV Guide*, November 11, 1995, pp. 15–16.

20. Gerosa, p. 200.

21. Winfrey, p. 18.

22. Reynolds, "A Year to Remember," p. 20.

23. *Oprah—Make the Connection*, Harpo Video, Inc., Buena Vista Home Video, 1997.

24. Ibid.

25. Bridget Kinsella, "The Oprah Effect," *Publishers Weekly*, January 20, 1997, p. 276.

26. Paul Gray, "Winfrey's Winners," *Time*, December 2, 1996, p. 84.

27. Kinsella, pp. 276–277.

28. "The Book Club, According to Oprah," *Newsweek*, October 7, 1996, p. 83.

29. Adam Cohen, "Trial of the Savory," *Time*, February 2, 1998, p. 77.

Chapter 10. Making a Difference

1. "Talk of the Future," *The New York Times*, September 16, 1997, p. E1.

2. Ron Stodghill, "Daring to Go There," *Time*, October 5, 1998, p. 84.

3. Harpo Productions press release, September 17, 1997, on the Internet on "Oprah Online," America Online (December 23, 1997).

4. Ibid.

5. Ibid.

6. *The Oprah Winfrey Show*, ABC-TV, April 14, 1997.

7. "Top of the List—the Most Fascinating Women of '96," *Ladies' Home Journal*, January 1997, p. 44.

8. Jonathan Van Meter, "Oprah's Moment," *Vogue*, October 1998, p. 392.

9. "Angry at Oprah," *The New York Times Magazine*, October 11, 1998, p. 19.

10. Van Meter, p. 327.

11. Patricia Sellers, "The 50 Most Powerful Women in American Business," *Fortune*, October 12, 1998, p. 82.

12. Mary-Ann Bendel, "TV's Super Women," *Ladies' Home Journal*, March 1988, p. 169.

13. Richard Zoglin, "Lady with a Calling," *Time*, August 8, 1988, p. 64.

14. Emma Bland, "How Oprah's Changed Our World, *McCall's*, November 1998, p. 70.

15. Harpo LIVE interview with Oprah Winfrey, June 10, 1997, on the Internet on "Oprah Online," America Online (August 27, 1997).

FURTHER READING

Adler, Bill, ed. *The Uncommon Wisdom of Oprah Winfrey: A Portrait in Her Own Words.* Secaucus, N.J.: Birch Lane Press, 1997.

Beaton, Margaret. *Oprah Winfrey: TV Talk Show Host.* Chicago: Children's Press, 1990.

Buffalo, Audreen. *Oprah Winfrey.* New York: Random House, 1993.

Greene, Bob, and Oprah Winfrey. *Make the Connection—Ten Steps to a Better Body and a Better Life.* New York: Hyperion, 1996.

King, Norman. *Everybody Loves Oprah.* New York: William Morrow and Co., Inc., 1987.

Mair, George. *Oprah Winfrey: The Real Story.* New York: Birch Lane Press, 1994.

Nicholson, Lois P. *Oprah Winfrey.* New York: Chelsea House Publishers, 1997.

Otfinoski, Steve. *Oprah Winfrey: Television Star.* Woodbridge, Conn.: Blackbirch Press, 1993.

Saidman, Anne. *Oprah Winfrey: Media Success Story.* Minneapolis: Lerner Publications Company, 1990.

INTERNET ADDRESSES

Harpo and ABC: *Oprah Homepage.*
<http://www.oprah.com> (September 17, 1998).

Jayne Scott Studios: *The Unofficial Guide to Oprah Winfrey.*
<http://www.jaynscott.com/oprah/> (September 17, 1998).

U.S. Department of Health and Human Services: "Spotlight on Ms. Oprah Winfrey."
<http://www.health.org/gpower/girlarea/gpguests/ OprahWinfrey.htm> (September 17, 1998).

INDEX